If I Could Raise My Kids Again

Books by William Coleman
from Bethany House Publishers

CHESAPEAKE CHARLIE SERIES
Chesapeake Charlie and the Bay Bank Robbers
Chesapeake Charlie and Blackbeard's Treasure
Chesapeake Charlie and the Haunted Ship

DEVOTIONALS FOR YOUNG CHILDREN
Animals That Show and Tell
Getting Ready for Our New Baby
If Animals Could Talk
Listen to the Animals
My Hospital Book
Singing Penguins and Puffed-Up Toads
Today I Feel Shy
What Children Need to Know When Parents Get Divorced

DEVOTIONALS FOR TEENS
Earning Your Wings

BOOKS FOR ADULTS
Before I Give You Away
Before Your Baby Comes
Eight Things Not to Say to Your Teen
It's Been a Good Year
Measured Pace
Newlywed Book
Ten Things Your Teens Will Thank You For . . . Someday
Today's Handbook of Bible Times and Customs
What Makes Your Teen Tick?

If I Could Raise My Kids Again

William L. Coleman

BETHANY HOUSE PUBLISHERS
MINNEAPOLIS, MINNESOTA 55438

If I Could Raise My Kids Again
Copyright © 1996
William Coleman

Published by Bethany House Publishers
A Ministry of Bethany Fellowship, Inc.
11300 Hampshire Avenue South
Minneapolis, Minnesota 55438

Printed in the United States of America.

Library of Congress Cataloging-in-Publication Data

Coleman, William L.
    If I could raise my kids again / William Coleman.
      p. cm.
    ISBN 1–55661–657–0 (pbk.)
     1. Parenting. 2. Parenting—Religious aspects—Christianity.
3. Parent and child. I. Title.
HQ755.8.C647   1996
248.8'45—dc20   96–4443
                                          CIP

*It takes wisdom to have a good family,
and it takes understanding to make it strong.*

Proverbs 24:3

WILLIAM L. COLEMAN is the well-known author of more than thirty Bethany House books on a variety of topics. Combining his experience as a pastor, researcher, writer, and speaker, he is noted for his effective communication in the area of family relationships and practical spirituality. He has been married for more than thirty years and is the father of three grown children.

Contents

A Note From the Author

As a young parent, lost and overwhelmed in the wilderness of child-raising, I often wondered how other people did it. How much was too much, how far was too far, and how little was too little?

I didn't want to hear a college professor explaining the latest theory on child psychology. Nor did I want to read about how white rats handle postpartum depression.

What I needed was a flesh-and-blood veteran parent who had been there. I wanted to talk to a mom who looked like she'd been up all night once or twice, and a dad who still had a twinkle in his eye because he remembered the good times. I needed a levelheaded person who was optimistic and loaded with common sense. I wanted a parent with some scars. Maybe a bite mark on his index finger. Possibly a dent on her chin from a misguided fork.

For those who have finished parenting, I believe the following chapters will ring true. We didn't all have the same experiences and yet, in a strange way, we did.

Most importantly, my hope is that this book will be as a veteran parent to help those who are presently in the parenting process. Help being the operative word, may this book help you realize you are normal. Help you pick up a few hints. Help you relish the happy days and occasions. Help you stay on course when the waves get rough.

I pray this book will allow you to see your children as one of life's great marvels. May it help you raise your voice to God in appreciation and thanksgiving for His good gifts.

It takes many people to make a book like this a reality. Gary and Carol Johnson and their staff at Bethany House have put their collective talents to work as we've put books together for almost twenty years. I'm grateful for the excellent job they do.

I also want to thank those children and parents who shared their observations, views, and vast experiences for this project.

I especially want to thank certain individuals. The parents of some of the children who grew up as best friends to our kids were most helpful as we sipped coffee, ate pie, and reminisced by the hour. Of course, I've changed the stories in the book enough to avoid embarrassing their children. My thanks to:

Chuck and Ruby Andersen,
Menno and Susanna Classen,
Don and Joyce Kupfersmith,
Val and Carol Oswald,
Treca Pritner, and
Syd and Patty Widga.

And again, thanks to my wife, Pat. If you know us, you realize that my books don't happen without her.

May these chapters build your courage and help you to enjoy your children. Have a good read.

Bill Coleman
Groundhog Day, 1995

1

The Grand Tour

Eventually every parent ends up taking a leisurely stroll around the old place. They don't plan to. It simply happens. It's the walk that maps out the journey you took with your children. In every room, down every hall, across the yard, and even in the garage you're bombarded with memories.

Young parents are in the middle of this journey. We older parents are happy for you because we know how rich, satisfying, and challenging the trip can be.

The storage room houses the crib our three babies—Mary, Jim, and June—slept in their first years. Each closet, stairway, and corner is a place where some wide-eyed child crouched playing hide-and-seek. As I walk by the dining room table, I can still picture our family playing games together. The twisting staircase is where June tripped and fell to the bottom, separating her shoulder. We still have the kitchen table where I sat many an hour, sometimes into the early morning, waiting for a teen who overstayed his or her curfew.

On the garage walls are the short hoes our children

used to work the fields each summer. Three or four old sleds are stacked in the rafters. Bicycle parts hang from the ceiling. Fishing gear fills one cabinet, and baseballs, footballs, tennis balls, and basketballs are crammed into another.

The backyard is filled with memories, too. We kicked the can, shot water pistols, and played trucks under the trees. It's where we had picnics, grilled burgers, and the children camped in the tent on summer nights. Mary and I planted the burning bush in this yard.

Parents don't spend much time taking tours through yesterday. These walks are hard on the heart and tighten the throat. But once in a while, we find ourselves drifting off and remembering.

Most of our memories are pleasant. They revolve around the people we love, and they help us recall how meaningful it all was.

While I was a parent-in-training, I ran across a couple of books that were helpful. They weren't technical types that told me why three out of four children don't like lima beans. They were practical and down to earth. The authors knew firsthand what it was like to have a toddler take the goldfish out of the bowl and play with them, to have a seven-year-old step on their glasses and crush them.

I am not big on theory, either, but I have had considerable experience. And that has left me with some knowledge that I'd like to pass on. This is how one parent did it, warts and all.

Knowledgeable Parents

Our lives often seem backwards. We try to put the swing set together, and only after we become frustrated enough do we read the instructions. By then the bars lean too far to the right, and dozens of leftover pieces are strewn across the yard. We hate to study how to do things, especially when we think the information should come naturally.

In the area of raising children, it might help to read some instructions first. Much will be learned day by day, but a few things could be weighed and considered ahead of time.

The present generation of parents is smarter this way. They aren't afraid to take classes, join support groups, and read books. Many have gone to their local churches, YWCA, or schools, and asked for help in becoming better parents.

The young parents I know are careful and concerned. They accept their children as precious gifts from God, and they are willing to seek knowledge and apply it to the skill of raising their kids. These parents are to be admired.

Be Encouraged

You as parents *are* up to the task. The Lord made us to reproduce and nurture children. So don't be ruled by your fears, but rise up to your hopes.

No one knows the future and none of us can guarantee how our children will "turn out." But our goal is to provide good values, protection, security, discipline, love, faith, and the many other qualities we ourselves possess and seek to develop in our own lives.

In the process, we'll get to know a few wonderful people—our own children.

2

Stand on the Chairs and Shout

My dad never praised me for anything. I can't remember him ever saying, "Good job" or, "You can do it."

It's not that he was mean or inconsiderate. Born before World War I, the last of thirteen children, my dad probably never heard a word of praise or gratitude from his parents, either.

Parents used to think it was wrong to praise their children. They thought it would weaken them somehow. They didn't want to turn their children into self-centered, big-headed sissies. Make them tough—boys and girls alike—was the theme.

As is the case with most of us, my dad was tied closely to the parenting skills he'd gleaned from his own boyhood home. He was bound to repeat the patterns and examples set before him.

Most men my age will say this is typical. Our dads didn't praise us for anything. And most of us didn't realize how much we were affected by this lack until we tried to praise our own children. The thoughts froze in our minds. The words became wedged in our mouths.

During our children's early years, I maintained the same standard of praise, or lack of it, as I'd known as a boy. While staying close to our children and involved in their lives, I was careful about what I said. When they excelled at something, I teased them about their accomplishments. That seemed like a good compromise. By teasing them, I brought attention to their abilities without making a big deal of it. What a bonehead I was!

The praise-less approach to parenting eventually leads to a crisis. A telephone call from a junior high counselor set a crisis in motion for me. He asked me to come to the school to discuss our daughter's test results. I went with fear and trepidation. My secret hope was that her ability would be a bit above average—not too high, of course, but not too low. Like the children in Garrison Keillor's *Lake Wobegon*: just above average.

The school counselor started out by explaining that Mary's mental abilities were indeed high. He said that by school standards she was in the category of students who should have no difficulty getting doctorate degrees if they chose to.

What terrific news! Her IQ was about 30 points higher than mine. At that moment, I felt very proud of my daughter.

After expressing my gratitude to the counselor for sharing this information, I left the building in a state of shock. I drove home in a trance. In my economy of values I thought: Mary must never know this. If she found out, she'd have no hope of ever being normal. I would protect Mary's right to be a bit above average. She would never become an egghead or some intellectual monster.

Her shame would be safe with me.

A week later, while out with a friend, I asked him if

he had a few minutes to hear me out. We drove to the park and I turned off the engine. Briefly, I described the details of my talk with Mary's counselor. I told him that I'd decided not to tell Mary about her giftedness.

"Are you nuts?" My friend got right to the point. "If your child were the football quarterback or batted .400, you'd be telling everyone about it. Now you feel embarrassed because she's intelligent? What a lousy attitude."

Reality hit like a ton of bricks. Of course Mary needed to know. In addition, she needed to be celebrated—a dinner out and special family recognition. She needed to know her options: She could go for her doctorate or run the cash register at Chuck's Drive-In—the choice was hers.

Each of us learns different lessons in life, and this was a big one for me. From then on I developed a new attitude toward praise and recognition. When our kids excelled at school, won a cross-country race, or got first chair in the band, we made fools of ourselves making a big deal of it.

We'd pull out the chairs at dinnertime and stand on them and shout! We'd cheer like schoolkids and make toasts with glasses of milk held high.

And when Mary finished law school and passed her bar exam, we stood on those same chairs.

Our only regret is that we didn't learn the principle of praise a bit earlier. We should have been standing on chairs when the children were preschoolers. We missed a lot of good parties and a good many laughs. We missed opportunities to encourage, lift up, and reinforce our kids in their early years.

The Bible tells us to "encourage one another daily" (Hebrews 3:13). I guess we must have thought the admonition was meant for encouraging missionaries and sick people, or women whose husbands were serving overseas. Well, it is, but it's also for parents. Encourage your children. Kids today live in a cold, hostile world, and they need all the praise they can get.

Parents who are afraid to praise their children are still out there. They are not confined to my generation. They are the tight-lipped, stern people who keep firm control over their emotions, cautious lest they burst into a fit of encouragement. It's a hard shell to crack. Often it takes the grace of God for some parents to let go and shout for joy. I've been there, and I know it wasn't easy for me.

Some of us grew up distrusting good news. We were suspicious of the ups. Every up must have a down, right? If we rejected the up in the first place, the down couldn't broadside us.

So we learned to live with the downs, eventually accepting them as life's norm. The sad part is, we may have passed that warped perspective on to our children.

I still struggle somewhat with good news. For example, if someone says something good about me, it frightens me. I don't like having attention called to myself. When the spotlight's on me, people will be able to see my faults.

Don't let it happen to your children. They deserve to hear good news about themselves. It should never be withheld from them.

The author of Ecclesiastes teaches us that "when times are good, be happy" (7:14). Don't resist good news. Accept it. Acknowledge it. Proclaim it.

Don't Praise Falsely

The fine line in this area is between false praise and genuine praise. Children who grow up on false praise learn that compliments can be empty and eventually painful. Never tell a child that he or she can jump across a canyon if they can't. It hurts too much when the child finds out the parent was only kidding—or worse yet, lying.

A professional baseball player tells this story: As a child his father practiced with him and they enjoyed playing together. His father made him feel like a million-dollar ballplayer.

Then while watching a game at Anaheim Stadium his dad pointed to Frank Tanana, California's fastball pitcher.

"Someday you'll be able to hit off that pitcher," his dad assured him.

The boy took it seriously. He assumed his father knew what he was talking about. The youngster practiced hard and eventually was signed to play ball in the minor leagues. And he was good. Extremely good.

One day his time came to bat against major league pitching. He picked up a bat, went to the on-deck circle, and waited his turn.

As he knelt in the dirt, the young man looked out at the mound. There stood Frank Tanana. In those days Tanana could throw a ball ninety miles an hour.

Whip! Whip! Whip! The youth watched in dismay as the balls, one by one, tore at him at high speed and into the catcher's glove.

Staring at the pitcher, the young man thought to himself, *My dad was wrong. I can't hit off this guy. There is no way.*

Fortunately, this rookie ballplayer went on to a long and excellent major-league career. But he never forgot the feeling he had that day when he realized his father had stretched the truth and left him disillusioned.

High Expectations

The young ballplayer's dad didn't actually lie to him, of course. In his mind, he could picture his son getting hits off any pitcher. A parent's dreams for his children are based on love and confidence in the child's ability. Children need parents who see a bright and happy future for them. Just be careful not to be too unrealistic.

Every parent wants to tell his child, "You can grow up to be anything you want to be." However, the painful truth is that is not necessarily so, and no amount of parent-speak will make it happen.

Do encourage your child to chase his own dreams and to broaden his horizons. Don't insist that a child champion any and every goal. Creating a false set of expectations frustrates and disappoints.

Praise has a downside when it's not true and honest.

When Mary was in college, I said to her, "You know, you might want to get your Ph.D. in English. Then you could teach in a small college and write books on the side."

She looked at me knowingly. "That's what you wish you'd done, isn't it?"

Ouch! I got caught trying to use praise to manipulate.

Emphasize the Positive

Somewhere we got the idea that the goal of parenting is to correct our children. If they get off-course, our job is to push, pull, or yank them back onto the proper path.

Sometimes that's exactly our task, and it needs to be done. On the other hand, encouragement will often do the job better than haranguing will.

My wife's Aunt Nell has the gift of encouragement. One day, when Pat was a child, she took it upon herself to straighten up one of the rooms in Aunt Nell's house. There were lots of small things out of place, and she spent a long time putting everything in perfect order.

The next day Pat found a cheerful note from Aunt

Nell, the angel of encouragement. She wanted Pat to know that someone had noticed her thoughtfulness and labor. These many years later, Pat still has that memory tucked away.

Children deserve thanks and encouragement when they do well. They know they're capable of doing wrong—that is often confirmed daily by parents, siblings, teachers, and even friends. They need to have the good things they do celebrated as often as possible.

When the infamous prodigal son returned from his wandering ways, his father held a feast and celebrated. There was a day when I wouldn't have reacted that way. I'd have considered such a time the perfect opportunity to lecture, to lay down the new rules, and to demand confession and true repentance.

But the prodigal's dad didn't do any of these things. He celebrated his son's return and let everyone in on the party. Who knows? He may have stood on a chair and shouted.

3

Aim for Respect Before Love

Those of you who grew up in a family where little or no love was expressed will want to keep that from being the case for your own children. Most of us desire to accomplish two things in this regard:

1. We want our children to feel loved.
2. We want our children to love us.

The first goal is admirable and clear. But danger lies in the second. A driving need to have our children love us is lined with peril. A parent's judgment is often seriously damaged by an overwhelming desire to be loved.

I always wanted my children to accept me, be with me, and join in whatever I did. That's certainly laudable. Who could fault a father for wanting to be close to his children? However, my need to find approval from my children frequently muddied the waters.

When it came to a simple exercise, such as playing a board game, I gave my son too much liberty in order to ensure his wanting to play with me the next time. He could pick the game, choose the time and place, and refuse to compromise with me or anyone else. I almost always went along with this because I craved closeness with my child.

I even realized at the time how crazy it was, but I rationalized that it was a small price to pay. I noticed other kids who would have nothing to do with their dads. My son *wanted* to be with me, and I was willing to do whatever it took to keep it that way.

Disguised as kindness, I can see it today for what it really was. Continuously giving in was really an act of selfishness on my part. Afraid of treating him too harshly, I swung too far in the opposite direction.

But the truth is, parents are generally crippled by two forces:

1. Our lack of understanding in raising kids.

2. Our personal needs (for love, control, independence, prestige, etc.).

Children both benefit and suffer from their parents' strengths and weaknesses. Wanting my son with me at any cost was one of my weaknesses. In the long run it was a serious disservice to him. He may not have suffered from neglect, but he was shortchanged, especially in the early years, by a doting father who never let him lose or discover the consequences of give-and-take.

Acting and Reacting

Instead of interacting with our children according to their needs, many of us merely act or react according to what our parents did.

My dad spent very little time with me, so the times we *were* together are etched forever on my memory. When my children came along, I didn't want to make the same mistakes my father had.

Therein lies the rub.

Trying to reinvent and correct the relationship my dad and I had, I was unfair to all three generations—his, mine, and my children's. My children needed to be accepted, loved, and taught one by one, as the individuals they are.

Parenting Is Not Re-created

Before we think we are the ones who will at last do it right, we must accept this fact: each generation does not re-create parenting. We are all limited to some extent by the parenting we received. And even though we won't parent exactly as our parents did, much of our efforts will be spent in repeating or reacting to what our parents did or didn't do while raising us. This does not mean we can't improve on the art, however.

We can learn about parenting from books and seminars, which involves our cerebral or cognitive understanding. The more visceral experience—the emotional, nonreasoning, gut-feeling response to life that comes from within—is learned from our childhood environment.

Parenting is a patchwork, then. We sew together pieces from our childhood experience, our acquired knowledge, our present environment, our spiritual exposure, input from our spouse, as well as other sources. We are the beneficiaries of these influences as well as their victims.

Into the mix comes the grace of God—if we allow it.

Respect and Love

Anyone who wants to learn more about love—all angles of it—will find plenty of material on the subject.

Books, tapes, seminars, sermons, and discussion groups are well within our reach in this day and age.

But if we want to study about respect, we could very well perish in some dusty library without a page of material.

Respect is a currently neglected subject in relational theology. Though the Bible speaks often of respect on the family level, the topic is seldom addressed.

Respect sounds cold, rigid, old-fashioned. Love sounds warm, giving, popular. But in reality, true love doesn't exist where there is no respect. I wish I'd known that fact earlier in life.

Scripture gives us these examples:

"The wife must respect her husband" (Ephesians 5:33).

"Children obey him [father] with proper respect" (1 Timothy 3:4).

"Show proper respect to everyone" (1 Peter 2:17).

"Each of you must respect his mother and father" (Leviticus 19:3).

And this is only a sampling. The Bible portrays respect as the cornerstone to basic relationships.

If parents aim for love and not respect, they are likely to reap contempt. If they aim for respect and not love, they may reap coldness. Better to aim for love and respect, respect defining the quality of love.

Keep the Balance

Children living with parents who don't respect each other see a warped kind of love. When a father claims to dearly love his wife but treats her like a person incapable of making a decision, it confuses his children. And when a mother says she loves her husband but ignores his wishes in the household, children are apt to question that love.

Children in this home love whom they pity instead of whom they respect.

It is fairly easy to train your children to love you because they can be manipulated by giving them everything they want. But respect isn't gained that way. Respect is earned when we don't play favorites, when we draw lines of limitation, and when we hold certain expectations for our children's behavior. The respected parent isn't afraid to be firm when necessary.

Love and respect your children and expect the same from them.

Don't Cloud the Issues

A proud grandfather sat on the floor with his cherished three-year-old grandson and watched him play, the boy seemingly just as contented to have his grandparent with him. But when Grandpa told the little fellow it was time to pick up his toys because they were about to leave, the lad totally ignored him.

"I said pick up the toys now," he repeated sternly.

The boy looked up coyly and said, "Grandpa, I don't like you anymore."

Without flinching, the grandfather replied, "I'm sorry to hear that, Tyler, because I really love you. But whether you like me or not, you're going to have to pick up your toys."

What maturity. Love wasn't the issue here, but obedience, and the grandfather was wise enough to keep it that way.

As most children his age, Tyler was clever enough to redefine the issue. He tried to shift the emphasis away from obedience and on to love. Being a natural psychologist, he looked for a vulnerable spot in his grandfather and hoped his desire to be loved was it.

Grandpa met Tyler head on. Some parents don't get that far. Too many would have made love the issue and picked up the toys, hoping to regain the child's affection. Skittish of conflict, adults who should know better take the servant role in hopes of winning their child's approval.

What is sacrificed in the process is respect. And without respect, love is diminished.

Discipline Garners Respect

One of the major roads leading to respect is discipline. But discipline that is too strict or unreasonable defeats the purpose. We're talking about a tricky art. Few of us discover the delicate balance between too much or too little.

The Bible tells us: "Moreover, we have all had human fathers who disciplined us and we respected them for it. How much more should we submit to the Father of our spirits and live!" (Hebrews 12:9).

Our family used to take turns doing dishes. (That was back when people actually washed dishes by hand.) From time to time each of the children had their own way of avoiding the inevitable. They suddenly had homework to do, errands to run, people to call. Sometimes nature called, or they were overcome by weariness. As parents, we usually held the line and demanded immediate compliance. Other times we were pussycats and fell for any flimsy excuse.

One Sunday afternoon, one of our daughters became particularly creative in her attempt to stave off her turn at the sink. Soon it was late afternoon, and then evening and time for youth group and church. After church she came rushing into the house like a volunteer with the fire department. Everyone was going to the next town for pizza; a car was waiting for her and she had to go immediately!

I told her, painfully, that she wasn't going anywhere. Painfully, because I didn't want my daughter to miss out on anything—especially not fun stuff. And painfully because I loved her so much and I wanted her to love me in return.

"Why not?" she shrieked, bent over as if suffering severe abdominal pain.

"Because you haven't done the dishes yet."

"I'll do them when I get back! No matter how late it is. I *pro*-mise."

"No, I think you should stay home and do them now."

Looking at me, her face twisted in agony, she asked the question I'll never forget, "*Why* are you doing this?"

It would have been more pleasant for me to bid her a happy evening and let responsibility slide. I wanted to see her pick the good fruit of life as much as the next dad. But she was losing respect—respect for her parents, respect for her own sense of duty, respect for her place in the family. At the risk of losing love, I knew I had to go for respect, and that sometimes only comes on the rocky road of discipline.

This story won't ring true to families who thrive on steady discipline. You won't identify if you have all your ducks in a row. But there are many of you out there, like me, who have trouble towing the line when it comes to discipline. How do you tell a child, "No, you can't," when inside your heart screams, "I really want you to"? How do you create a boundary when you want your child to go a bit beyond the boundaries into a fuller life?

You do it painfully. Later you realize you did the right thing. Your kids may even look back with gratitude. They may even love you for it.

Respect Your Child

You're not likely to gain respect from your child unless you show respect. In past generations some considered children unworthy of respect. Some adults still look at children as nonpeople.

One woman recounted her childhood to me in these terms:

> As a child my parents held no regard for anything I was involved in. If I asked a friend to come over at three o'clock, for instance, my parents could change my plans at any moment for any reason, even if I'd received permission ahead of time.
>
> If I was watching a television show, my dad would walk into the room and without a word change the channel to something else. After all, I was only a child. Whatever I was watching was unimportant.
>
> My parents had no respect for me as a child or for any of my interests. I think that's one of the reasons why I have so little respect for them to this day.

Respect for your children should be high on your priority list. In turn, your children will grow up to respect you, as well as appreciate and value each individual, young or old.

4

Let Them Pull the Cat's Tail

The parents I've talked to don't want to see their children get hurt. What reasonable adult would want his child to suffer pain? We want good things for our kids—satisfying experiences, and endless happiness.

On the surface that sounds wonderful, but there may be a limit to this kind of logic. The happiness of our children may have become a modern obsession. For some of us, every twist and turn in our lives has become an attempt to please our children and keep them from discomfort.

Pat's Cats

Mark Twain is reported to have said something to the effect that he never tried to stop someone from picking up a cat by its tail. He said the educational value alone was well worth the experience.

More children need to pick up a cat by its tail, and more parents need to let them.

My wife, Pat, loves animals and cares dearly for the

two cats that live at our house. My personal affection for these critters is considerably more reserved. In keeping with Pat's loving nature, one day she decided to give the cats a bath.

She drew the water in the bathtub and then gently coated Bart's large body with shampoo. The cat seemed a little confused, but nothing prepared Pat for what happened when she carefully placed the furry feline into the warm water.

I arrived home to see long bloody scratches down my wife's arms. Bart was perched atop the radiator, darting his suspicious eyes at anyone who dared approach him.

Maybe someone should have told Pat that cats don't like baths (at least not one given by someone other than themselves). But, I ask you, who could have talked her out of it? She thought she was doing a loving thing. In any case, her educational experience was so thorough, no one will ever have to talk her out of it again.

Not that we want our children (or our wives, for that matter) to get hurt. But overprotection has an injury factor of another kind.

Risks Must Be Taken

Eventually our children have to
    waste some money
    flunk some tests
    taste spoiled milk
    miss the school bus
    get bored
    get ripped off
    be dumped by a friend
    fall down
    drop their gum in the dirt
    and experience other unfortunate setbacks.

In most cases, the sooner it happens the better. Children need to sample both the setbacks and the rewards of life. They need to know that neither Mom nor Dad will always be there to kiss them and make it better, or to pull them out of a jam.

This is not to suggest that parents should become cold and unfeeling, but certainly realistic.

Bail Out Time

Like any other parent, I have bailed my children out of bad situations. Sometimes it was the right thing to do. Other times, I admit I made serious mistakes. Looking back, I wish I'd allowed them to sink or swim more often. The catchy part is having the wisdom to know when. No one can tell you when to let your child learn on his own and when to bail him out, but both must happen. You have to find the balance.

The Bible presents two principles along this line.

Principle Number One. Parents normally know how to give good gifts to their children (Luke 11:11–13).

Moms and Dads enjoy doing good things for their kids. Even more so, our heavenly Father gives good gifts to His children.

Principle Number Two. Let your child find out some things for himself. The prodigal son's father let his son grab the cat's tail (Luke 15:11–12). He allowed the young man to go off on his own, even though he knew there would be pain and regret down the road.

These two checkpoints lead to sanity. Be good to your child *and* let him experience some pain.

The Birthday Truck

Four-year-old Austin received a large blue truck for his birthday. His parents knew their son would enjoy hauling dirt in the backyard with it. Every day Austin experienced hours of pleasure making roadways and moving earth from place to place.

One day, for some unknown reason, Austin angrily smashed his prized truck against a tree. The plastic wheels flew off and the rear of the truck was badly dented.

His parents, who witnessed the incident, had to make a quick judgment call. They wrestled with their spontaneous emotions. Should they lecture their son about the evils of smashing his toy, and later replace it? Should they tell Austin where to find tape or glue to repair the truck himself? Should they offer to pay for half of a new truck and subtract the other half from his meager resources? Or should they simply leave Austin alone with the results of his anger?

Whatever they decided, they had to weigh this question: How can we fairly allow our child to feel pain for his actions? It is interesting to note that most adults would agree that these parents needed to let Austin feel some pain. That is, of course, until those adults have children of their own and are dedicated to protecting them from pain!

Throwing Away Responsibility

In today's newspaper there was a story about a teenage girl who obviously never learned about the relationship between her actions and the inevitable consequences. Reportedly afraid that her mother would discover her pregnancy, the girl went to great lengths to disguise her condition. When she gave birth, she tossed the baby out of a second-story window!

Fortunately, someone heard the discarded child crying and stopped to investigate. The baby suffered skull fractures, hypothermia, and dehydration. Medical officials said that if the baby had not been found, it could not have survived long in the frigid weather.

A police officer said the young mother simply wasn't thinking rationally. She just wanted out of her predicament.

Minds in panic situations may be hard to understand. It would appear that the teenager could not at that moment draw a line connecting her actions to the consequences the baby would suffer. And then again, maybe she could.

All children need to grow up understanding that their actions have consequences. When a child cracks a window or loses his money, the parent too often is quick to replace the broken window or the lost money. The message given is that no one is accountable, nothing is truly lost, materials and supplies are inexhaustible.

Adults who were raised this way often have trouble getting to work on time, paying their bills, or remaining faithful to their spouses. They don't expect their actions to have consequences that are directly tied to them.

Forgiveness, restoration, and second chances are important, but the primary lesson here is that our behavior has an effect on the people and things around us.

No one can know the grace of forgiveness until they've fallen short. If a child feels that no harm is ever done, he can't grasp the need for forgiveness.

By "kissing" everything and making it better, we stunt the natural maturing process. A child won't see that his actions affect others for good or bad. Denied that knowledge, he is unable to see the ripple effect of his behavior on the total scheme of things.

Love and Accountability

Some parents feel that if they love a child, they won't call him into accountability. They define love as a blindly tolerant emotion, with few, if any, boundaries. In reality, love is true love only if it has borders. Love that allows an individual to do anything, anytime, no matter how harmful, isn't truly love.

Love must say:

You spilled it; you clean it up.

You got the tools out; you put them back.

You broke it; you pay for it (within reason).

Sometimes it can't be done. The age of the child, his physical abilities, and his financial resources enter in. But when possible, the culprit must be made responsible for the consequences of his misdeed.

God loves us in an unconditional manner, and yet He holds us accountable. Not a bad pattern to follow. The author of Romans tells us, "So then, each of us will give an account of himself to God" (14:12).

Granted, Christ has paid our penalty; but God still holds us responsible for the damage we do. We can't pass it off and say someone else made us do it.

A prosecutor handling a murder case told the jury the defendant was definitely guilty. True, he explained, this man was abused as a child. No one contests that. But communities are filled with hundreds, if not thousands, of adults who were abused. Yet they hold themselves in check and do not murder people.

People who don't take responsibility for their actions soon develop a victim mentality. It's the thinking that we don't ever cause anything bad to happen; others always cause bad things to happen to us.

If we teach our children that they are merely victims of society, we place a curse on their lives. They need to grow up knowing that they are capable of causing both good things and bad things to happen.

The natural progression of responsibility should work this way:

If a baby spills milk, mother or father cleans it up.

If a young child spills milk, mother or father helps the child clean it up.

If an older child spills the milk, the child cleans it up.

When parents realize that they are still cleaning up after someone who is capable of doing it themselves, they have interfered with the natural progression of responsibility. Those parents will most likely look back with regret. And so will the child.

When a teenager comes home and tells her mother that she's pregnant and that it's her parents' fault, she clearly sees herself as a victim instead of accountable for her own actions.

Children who are allowed to suffer the consequences of their behavior are less likely later in life to blame others for the undesirable circumstances they find themselves in.

5

Spend More Time Together

For a little more than a year, I had a part-time job driving a flower delivery truck. My responsibilities took me into small towns, villages, and the only two big cities in Nebraska. Each morning I loaded up pots of Swedish ivy, azaleas, and carnations and whisked them off to supply the floral shops of our land.

When the children's schedules allowed it, I let them take turns riding along with me for the day. I found that two or three of them together didn't work. It was too crowded, and none of them felt particularly special. Each child wanted the individual attention that was possible when I took only one of them. Each wanted to feel like the king or queen for a day.

Pat would put some goodies together for us to eat along the way, but I insisted that she not pack lunch. At noon my passenger got to choose the fast-food restaurant where we'd dine. That was big time in those days.

The two of us would work together all day. My helper would carry in pots or look behind the vehicle to help me back up. Afternoons were spent checking out the ice cream stands. We had our favorites in Franklin, Broken Bow, and in far-off North Platte.

One of our more exciting memories was when I was driving through downtown Lincoln and hung a sharp left. Cars peeled in every direction as we barreled the wrong way down a one-way street. For years that was one of the children's favorite stories whenever a conversation got around to the old flower truck.

I have only two or three memories like that with my own dad. One time we walked across the Capitol grounds in Washington, D.C., and stopped to eat omelettes at a restaurant on Pennsylvania Avenue. We never fixed a light switch together or tried our hand at plumbing. He always had places to go and things to do—without me. Whenever I asked him where he was going, he'd brush me off with the lame reply, "I'm going to see a man about a dog."

At the time, I had lots of needs and gaps to fill in my life. I only wish he could have been around a little more to help connect the dots.

Some, who grew up on farms, have memories of being required to do too much work. Others, like my wife, Pat, have the fondest memories of working on the farm together with her father, whom she adored.

More Than Money

If you had parents who did their best to support you through your growing-up years, you can be grateful. As we become adults and have families of our own, we realize how hard it is to earn enough money to care for a wife and children and still spend time with them. That is especially true today with the increased standard of living that seems forced upon us.

The business of supporting a family sometimes means less time together, but togetherness doesn't have to be all fun and games. Working on projects, fixing, maintaining, even hanging out together has great value. It's the nearness, the sharing of the experience, the identity, and the belonging that makes it worth the doing.

Grandparents Are Great at Togetherness

Pat remembers spending time with her grandmother on the eastern shore of Maryland. Together they sewed, shelled peas, rolled out biscuits, picked wild blueberries, and made delicious cobblers.

Her grandmother wasn't "in charge" of the entertainment committee. They accomplished things together and enjoyed it.

That influence passed on to the next generation. When we bought our first home, each of the children had their own small bedroom. The kids picked out their own individual wallpaper, paint colors, and carpet. They each helped to decorate their own rooms.

I remember Mary chose Holly Hobbie wallpaper, and she and her mother worked together making the room just how Mary wanted it to be.

As they grow older, some children don't want to be seen doing anything, anytime, with their parents, and often it is wise for parents to encourage their teenagers to find work outside the home. But whenever togetherness is possible, and for as long as possible, it is worth every minute, and will be fondly remembered by both parent and child.

Alien Parents

At an increasing rate, kids are becoming disconnected from who their parents are and what they do. Many parents leave early in the morning and return late at night. Exactly where they go and what they do remains a mystery to most children.

Entire communities have been built an hour and a half to two hours away from large cities. Many parents make that long trip twice a day to pursue lucrative careers at the sacrifice of time with their children. They provide material things for their kids, but little togetherness. The best they can do is try to put in quality time on the weekends.

If you are forced, out of necessity, to spend more time away from your children than you'd like to, don't become distant from their true needs. Be alert, and look for ways to fill those emotional and physical gaps.

Projects to Share

Many parents do their best to provide togetherness. Take a look around the parks, lakes, lumberyards, malls, homes, and see how many mother/daughter, father/son teams (or alternate combinations) are actually doing things together.

I've seen them skeet-shooting, working on cars, sewing projects together, and cooking up a storm. Though there are many who fail at this togetherness, there are those who shine, too.

The day after Thanksgiving, I went downtown in search of my wife and daughter. Not knowing exactly where to find them, I dashed in and out of several stores. One store I entered didn't have another male shopper in it. I saw lots of females shopping in pairs. Most of these were obviously mothers and daughters. The place was packed, and they seemed to be enjoying each other's company. Even if they'd missed some valuable times together before, they were certainly making up for it now.

Sharing Means Being Together

One of the most familiar Scripture passages about child/parent relationships is Deuteronomy 6:6–9. These verses describe a way to pass on our spiritual values. The methods outlined are all based on togetherness.

"Impress [the commandments] on your children. Talk about them when you sit at home and when you walk along the road, when you lie down and when you get up."

Talking, sitting, walking, lying down, and getting up all presuppose close proximity. We aren't told to share spiritual values while we're away at board meetings or while we're working overtime or taking graduate classes. The transference of spiritual values is done best while we're together, doing everyday things.

Our children will never thank us for this, nor should they. If we turned down a promotion to spend more time with them, they don't ever need to know that. If Mom gave up a career so she could be home with her young children, that's her business. If Dad refused to be president of the club so he could be home more, that's his call to make.

Parents don't expect medals. In fact, they are foolish to beg for appreciation or recognition. Parents who sacrifice (and most parents do) don't do it for applause.

Smart parents aim for closeness because it's right. Togetherness is filled with merit of its own. It's all right if our children never understand the sacrifices we might make. Parents make them because they love their children.

Lasting Values

If you wonder who voted for Jimmy Carter for President, you've met one of his fans. I did, and I'm glad I did. I voted for him twice, and if given the opportunity, I would vote for him again. There, I've said it.

When our children were quite young we took them to a Carter-for-President rally, and they shook hands with the Christian gentleman. The press happened to take our picture together and pasted it on the front page of the local newspaper.

When fall came, each class at school held mock elections, and our children voted. It wasn't until years later that they told us the results of that election.

"How do you think it felt, Dad," Mary said, "to know there was only one vote cast in my class for Carter, and that vote was cast by a Coleman? And in Jim's class, too, Carter got only one vote. And in June's class—just one vote! How does that make you feel, Dad?"

"Wonderful! Magnificent!" I said. "You picked up values from your parents, because we were around enough to share those values." Most of the time we shared our political views, and other significant views and values with our kids, around the dinner table.

Our grown children don't share all of our views and choices and are free to say so. They also aren't afraid to hold on to a viewpoint, even if they hold it alone. If they are the only one who supports a cause, they still support it. They know it doesn't take a majority to make something right.

Fortunately, they have had the opportunity to see a value system at work, complete with flaws.

Many Don't Want to Be at Home

While some parents feel frustrated that they can't spend more time with their children, there are many out

in the workplace who don't want to be at home. Some
have carved out schedules specifically designed to keep
them busy. Yet those same people will complain about
not having time to give to their children! Is it guilt?

Years ago I wrote an article entitled "Pastor, Go
Home." I suggested that pastors should stop going so
many places and doing so many things without their
families.

The response was immediate, and much of it was
negative. Pastors assured me that God had called them
to sacrifice their time, and, if need be, their families!

The fact is, a lot of people who don't go home at normal hours don't want to be there.

A woman became very angry with me when I suggested that many of us work too many hours in order to
purchase too many things.

I listened to a speaker tell a group of men at a seminar
how he explained to his son that the Lord expected him
to participate in events such as these. He wished he
could do more things with his son, but he really had no
choice in the matter. No choice? I remember thinking at
the time, *There isn't one thing going on at this conference worth ignoring our sons and daughters for.* Sometimes we need to be away, but not nearly as much as
some of us think we do.

In Lee Iacocca's book *Talking Straight** the former
vice-president of Ford and president of Chrysler described his attitude toward family this way:

"There's always the excuse of work to get in the way
of the family. I saw how some guys at Ford lived their
lives—weekends merely meant two more days at the office. That wasn't my idea of family life. I spent all my
weekends with the kids and all my vacations."

---

*New York: Bantam Books, 1989, p. 27.

One of the few certainties in life is that we'll look back and wish we'd spent more time enjoying our children. More family togetherness is a goal worth pursuing.

6

Find a Church Life

On Christian radio call-in shows, it's not uncommon to hear a mother calling in with a question like this: "My daughter is sixteen years old, and she wants to stop going to church. Do you think I should let her?"

Millions of parents with small children are headed for this dilemma. They raise their children happily through the nursery, through the Sunday school classes of the grade school years, and then the age of teendom sweeps over them like a flood.

If a young person hasn't tied in to the local church in a meaningful way by age sixteen, he most likely will begin to spread his wings at this point.

When Jesus Christ and the church are of paramount importance to a parent or parents, they are crushed to see their child reject what they hold to be the core of life.

Questions to Ask Early On

While your children are still walking around with a bottle in one hand and pulling up their diaper with the other, ask yourselves a couple of questions about the church you attend.

(1) Does our church minister to the individual needs of children and young people?

(2) If not, can we together with other parents get our church moving in that direction?

If the answer to either of these questions is yes, settle down and relax. You're on the family track.

But if the answer to both questions is no, it's time to move on and not look back. If your church isn't a family-oriented church, it doesn't deserve your family's attendance.

Church is where children get their first impression of what Christianity is all about. Does this church fit your family's needs? Can you work together with others in the congregation to see that it does meet your family's needs?

When you choose a church, you're choosing where you and your family will serve Christ, grow, and develop in the Christian faith. It is where you will invest your time, energy, and resources.

One of our grown daughters and her family began to attend a church where soon afterward the congregation dismissed the pastor. This was a hard time for them, but they decided to stay because they felt it was a good church in which to raise children.

Before attending any church, it's not too much to ask if the church is a good place for your entire family.

If you were a child or teenager and had the choice, would you voluntarily attend your church? Some parents don't think this is a choice for a ten-year-old to make, but young people form their concept of church quite early and tend to hold on to it throughout life.

Too many children are dragged off to a church every week where they are totally turned off by the sermon, the music, and the order of service. After sixteen years of zoning out on Sunday mornings, it's no wonder they want to stay home.

Recently I asked a group of local church leaders this question: "If a child or young person told you he was totally bored in your church service, how would you respond?"

Every leader who answered implied it would be the child's own fault if he was bored. They would tell the child or youth to straighten up and pay better attention. Not one leader suggested that the service be reevaluated!

What they were saying, in essence, was that the service met the needs of adults, or at least the leaders. It was high time the children got with the adult program.

I wouldn't take my family to a church in the business of training children to tune out and still call it worship.

As a father, when my children were young, it was my responsibility to find a place where they could be effectively ministered to. Sometimes I met that obligation and other times I failed. But if I had it to do over again, I would put a lot more effort into making the right choices concerning where we worshiped and served God.

Other Support Systems

Most parents are thankful for the parachurch groups that minister to their children. In our case, we found two youth programs that had positive effects on our kids.

The first was Travel Camp. A local youth organization took a busload of teens to faraway places each summer for ten days. They went to the Grand Canyon, Yellowstone Park, even Canada, tenting all the way.

These short, fun-filled, spiritually packed journeys were extremely beneficial to our children. We salute the adults who gave of themselves to have a meaningful influence on our teens. From our viewpoint as parents, this was an excellent connection that made our children feel good about being Christians.

The same was true of the once-a-week morning Bible studies. It was a happy place where young people could join other teens in a large group and know they weren't alone in their faith.

Christian camps are also high on my list of effective programs for youth. Our children attended and, when they were old enough, all three worked at various camps. The influence was strong and positive. Occasionally they met a counselor or two who interjected his own political views or pushed his opinions too hard, but the benefits of the camp experience far outweighed the other factors.

Be Honest

When a church is strong in sound teaching and models basic Christian life principles, point out these advantages to your children. But if a church is boring, don't try to fool your kids. They aren't dumb, and they soon give up on adults who deny reality.

It's far better to admit there's a problem and discuss what might be done about it. We need to be honest with a young person if we are concerned about a lack in the church and would like to do something about the situation.

A pastor of a large church in Georgia told a young mother he'd appreciate her stopping by to express her concerns about the youth program. The church already had a sports program and other ways to relate to youth, but if there was something else he could do, the pastor wanted to hear about it.

Many pastors feel this way. They want to hear from interested parents, and they sincerely want to meet the needs of their youth.

Back to the Question

What about the sixteen-year-old we mentioned earlier who didn't want to go to church anymore? How should her parents respond?

Try this compromise: If she's willing to attend another Christian church, she should be allowed to go. At sixteen, her parents have the right to tell her she can't stay home, but neither does she necessarily have to attend her parents' church.

Her family's church has had sixteen years to connect with this young lady. It may not be entirely the fault of the local church, but the connection didn't happen. If the teen seems mature enough to spread her wings a bit on her own, let her find a place of fellowship where she might more easily see the presence of Christ.

Many teens simply want to exercise a little independence. Why not allow them that liberty in a controlled and safe environment? If they aren't given any choices, soon the drive to choose becomes an obsession. They may try to link up with a questionable or dangerous religious group just to prove that their parents can't control them.

Years ago two teenage boys asked for permission to visit other churches. The pastor got wind of it and blew a corpuscle. According to him, that was a dangerous choice for young people to make alone.

Eventually the parents decided to let their boys go ahead and try it. They were given six weeks to visit other churches, bringing a bulletin home from each, and a willingness to discuss and evaluate the differences among them.

On the fifth Sunday the boys slipped quietly back into a pew at their parents' church. They needed to know they were free to attend any church they cared to, but given the freedom, they realized how good their family church was and chose to stay there.

Church Attendance Is Not Enough

Unfortunately, it wouldn't take long to make a list of kids who grew up in a church but today have wandered far from it. Sometimes their absence has little to do with their parents, or the church they attended.

Church attendance alone is not enough, of course, but it is a key to God's design in helping His family grow, develop, and stay close to Him. The most important factor in the life of a Christian is his relationship with Jesus Christ.

One of our main functions as parents is to provide an opportunity for our children to get valuable Christian teaching and fellowship. In later years, each young person will have to decide for himself how he will respond to that good influence.

Social Life

The social benefits that naturally come from being in a church fellowship shouldn't be treated lightly. We can't choose our children's friends, but that doesn't mean we can't have some input. Through the church, parents have the opportunity to provide an atmosphere where their children are more likely to associate with other Christians and develop positive and meaningful friendships.

If we want our children to hang out with Christian friends, we must make it possible for them to move in circles where Christian young people are found. Vibrant, relevant churches with true spiritual life are ideal places for Christian youth to relate to others in their age group.

Our family remembers the churches where we definitely felt we belonged. Adults and older children alike knew our kids as friends. They carried all three of them around when they were small and sat with them during services and special events. During the week the children from our congregation played together in each other's homes.

In many ways the church has been like an extended family for us. We trusted one another and benefited from each other's company.

A church filled with caring people who love the Lord is simply a good place for a family to be.

7

Learning From Our Children

Our firstborn was a girl. Little Mary taught me more about the value of women than a hundred groups of feminists carrying banners and declaring their rights.

God brought this beautiful, bright daughter into our lives while I was in my last year of graduate school. She taught me more about life than any part of my long educational experience.

After a hard day of school and work I'd return to our small mobile home, and the first thing I did was bundle up Mary and hold her. Looking at that small brown-eyed infant, I would think, *Who says girls aren't as smart as boys? Who says there are some careers closed forever to my daughter? Who says they'd rather have their firstborn be a male?*

I remember thinking about the fact that female babies are destroyed in a large part of this evil world. They are often aborted merely because of their gender. They are drowned, left exposed in deserts, and sold into prostitution.

When those parents looked into the soft, innocent faces of their tiny daughters, didn't they see what I saw? Didn't they see the love, trust, and dependence that I saw in Mary's eyes?

When Mary came into my world, my whole gender outlook changed overnight. God sent her to teach this stubborn male. And she did it without saying a word.

Seen and Not Heard

When we were raising our kids, two theories were still prevalent.

(1) Children were to be seen and not heard.

(2) Children were empty personalities waiting for their parents to mold, make, and shape them.

In effect, children were nonpeople. When they reached twenty-one, then they were considered a true person.

Imagine how bewildered we were when our children came bouncing into our home ready to teach—complete with their own curriculum, lesson plans, and teaching aids. They were on a mission from God. School was in session from the day they checked in, and classes were conducted year-round. Their parents were the students.

Individualism

Jim and June taught us about individualism. Every person has to be handled differently. What was good for Mary wasn't necessarily the right approach for Jim or June.

Jim always wanted to swim upstream. Not because it was easier but because it was different. All the input in the world by any number of people could not stop him from following his own trails.

Not to be outdone, June cut her own path as well. From the day we brought her home from the hospital she did it her way. She didn't want to be held and cuddled like the others and she let you know it in no uncertain terms.

As she got older, June decided she would be the family musician, even though there didn't seem to be any musical genes in the clan. By the time she was in high school, she was an award-winning pianist, a flutist, and a soloist.

Where did the talent come from? Not from us! Only June and God know the answer to that one. June was not one to wait around for someone to "mold, make, and shape" her.

It is a profound fact of life that every person is a unique individual. If God doesn't make two snowflakes alike, why would He create two identical people?

Therefore, God didn't create billions of people. Rather, He created billions of individuals. Apparently, the Lord thought the gamble of individualism was worth the price.

Many still don't believe in it. They want to tie down a child and control his every move. They want to guarantee the outcome of the product. My children taught me how foolish that kind of thinking is.

Start Counting

One of the books I read early on about parenting was written by Charlie Shedd. In it he suggests the count system for discipline. If a child fails to do what is expected of him, the parent should simply announce, "You have until I count to four (or more, depending on the task) to get that done." Don't tell him what the consequences are, just start counting. The child responds quickly to the pressure.

Great advice. Exactly what I was looking for at the time.

When Mary refused to go to bed at the appointed hour, I would start counting. "One . . ."

"I can't find my shoes," she would protest.

"Two . . ."

"Where is my teddy bear?" she whined.

"Three . . ."

Mary disappeared to her bed. Every time.

With Jim it was the same. By three he was gone.

Then June came along.

The day arrived, when she was about three, that she refused to go to bed. I knew it was time for the count system.

"All right, June, you've got till the count of four to get to your room. One . . ."

June backed up against the wall.

"Two," I continued unabated.

June crouched down and made two fists.

Her body language said, "Come on, Dad, give it your best shot."

School was in session. June taught me that everyone is different. What works well for one child may fail miserably with another. How foolish of me to think a child is a child is a child.

Giving Toys Away

Do you recall the first time your child gave a toy away on his own? He may have had an extra truck and gave it to the neighbor kid. Your daughter may have given a doll.

How did you react? You probably told your little one to march next door and get that toy back, this minute. You probably thought, *Does this kid think money grows on trees? Doesn't he appreciate our gifts to him?* Sure he does. That's why he gave it away. He thought you were supposed to give gifts to the people you liked.

As parents, we understand the price of a toy, but we often lose sight of its value. The true value of a thing isn't realized until we lose it—or give it away.

Not to worry. As your children grow into adults, they'll learn that grown-ups hang on to things. A man's worth is measured by what he collects and hoards, not by what he gives away.

Let your children teach you the spirit of generosity.

Lessons in Forgiveness

Children teach by example.

Your daughter comes home crying. Sally has thrown sand in her face and she is terribly upset.

You hustle the distraught child into the bathroom and wash her hands and face.

"Well, I'm not surprised," you say. "I've never trusted that family. Her Uncle Fred is something else, and her stepfather..."

Handing your daughter a towel, you head for the telephone. You will call Sally's mother and tell her what her child did.

Meanwhile, your daughter slips quietly back outside to play with Sally!

Children understand that friends sometimes throw sand in your face. It hurts and you feel insulted. But you shake it off, forgive them, and go back to play again.

Adults, on the other hand, plot and plan to get even. They tell everyone else about it and keep the problem hot.

We often miss the lessons God sends our way because they are taught by our children.

Our Children Are on Loan

As we cradled our firstborn in our arms, we assumed she belonged to us. We thought we would have this daughter in our possession for the rest of our lives.

Were we in for an education!

Almost immediately Mary began to separate herself from us. She wanted to do things her own way and in her own time. Eventually the truth dawned on us. Mary would spend the rest of her life seeking her own identity and being different from her parents.

We thought we owned her, like buying a car. We soon learned otherwise. Children are on loan to us, and almost immediately we have to start giving them back.

We must let them go so they can become what God wants them to be. Any attempt to keep them for ourselves is a violation of the agreement.

It's a hard lesson. I wanted to put them in jars with holes punched in the lid. But the Lord said, *Let them go, they aren't yours to keep.*

Once we understood that, our goals changed. We started preparing our children to leave instead of trying to smother them and keep them with us. Everything we did was aimed for the front door, and how we could make today the best possible.

There are still times, even now that they are grown, when I wish I could sweep them into my arms again. I wish I could push them in a swing or eat burgers with them on a beach at the Platte River. I wish I could take June to one more spelling bee. Shoot BBs one more time with Jim, or take Mary on another date.

But my lease is up. We can do other things together,

but my days as an overseeing parent are over.

Seize the moments you have together with your young children.

What Time Does School Start?

Jesus knows that children are excellent teachers. That's why He tells us to look to them to learn about God.

Our children were grown before I realized they were sent to be my personal tutors. If I were a new parent today, I'd show up each morning with my mental notebook. Then I'd ask the Lord to make me an alert student—to show me what I could learn from my teacher-in-a-crib about trust, love, caring, faith, patience, dependence, independence, forgiveness, and whatever else He wanted me to know.

I'd start taking notes as each child made his or her appearance. And I'd keep attending classes through their grade school years, the teen years, and on into adulthood.

There are some truths so wise and so deep that God is reluctant to entrust them to adults. Read that again. Then look at what Jesus said in Luke 10:21. "I praise you, Father, Lord of heaven and earth, because you have hidden these things from the wise and learned, and revealed them to little children. Yes, Father, for this was your good pleasure."

Does Jesus mean God reveals these things to children, or to adults who are childlike? There isn't enough difference there to worry about. Anyone with the kind of faith a child possesses can understand many of the Lord's most profound teachings.

Keep an eye on your child. He may know some things about God that you've long forgotten.

In the same vein, Jesus Christ told us to learn about

personal faith by watching children. They—especially the little ones—seem to know more about believing and trust than most adults do.

"I tell you the truth, unless you change and become like little children, you will never enter the kingdom of heaven" (Matthew 18:3).

You don't learn that in parenting classes. You learn about faith by watching your children.

The angels in heaven, who are in close contact with God, are constantly looking after the little ones. They live closer to the angels than we parents do.

"See that you do not look down on one of these little ones. For I tell you that their angels in heaven always see the face of my Father in heaven" (Matthew 18:10).

Children are capable of praising God for who He is and for what He does. Little tykes are very accepting, trusting, and guilelessly grateful.

"From the lips of children and infants you have ordained praise" (Matthew 21:16).

While I was raising my children, I seldom thought of them as my teachers, but when I look at my grandchild, it seems quite obvious. Children are key instructors for those who are open to what God wants to say.

8

Give Them More Choices

Nowadays schools offer classes in decision-making. Students are given lots of options and are encouraged to make choices. The theory behind the classes is that young people need more experience making choices and decisions before they enter the difficult and unpredictable adult world.

Children will suffer from choice deprivation if their parents try to pick and choose everything for them, but there's a strong temptation to program our children. We want them to take piano lessons, go to volleyball camp, join Little League, take gymnastics, and get a paper route, because we know what's best for them. Sometimes we do know what's best. Sometimes we make choices that don't begin to fit their personalities.

Jim must have been in fifth or sixth grade when the Sunday school superintendent called to ask why he wasn't at practice for the Christmas program. She evidently couldn't understand his lack of driving passion to play the part of a donkey or to pretend to be a guiding star.

"Well, thanks for calling," I replied in my most understanding tone. "I'll check with Jim and see if he wants to participate."

"Frankly, Mr. Coleman," she said sternly, "I think the real question is whether or not *you* want Jim in the Christmas program."

The superintendent's response caused me to do a great deal of pondering. Should participation in the Christmas program really have been a parental decree? By the same token, should a child take lessons on a band instrument if the only one who wants him to do it is the parent? And should children be forced to join an athletic team if they have no personal interest in it? How much should adults influence their children's present and future by making decisions for them?

When Do We Begin?

Parents normally pose this question in one form or another: At what age should I "let go" of my children? Most expect the answer to range somewhere between eighteen and twenty-five.

Letting go, in its best form, is a process. Too often we look at it as a gate—one that remains closed until a particular day when it is opened. That's why we look for a date/age formula for letting go. But with children we need to think "process." Letting go and letting them make choices increases each year until they become young adults and make all of their own decisions.

Human Dignity

Prisoners' choices are restricted to a minimum. They are kept in cells, have limited visiting hours, and have no choice in what they wear or eat. Patients in mental hospitals, of necessity, are given few decisions to make.

When human beings are able to choose for themselves what they want and where they will go, they rise up to enjoy the dignity God gave them. The Lord gave Adam and Eve the power to make decisions, even though the result proved disastrous.

Our goal should be to raise a child to be an adult who can function as a free moral agent. Eventually this agent must be responsible for his own mistakes and successes.

There is a fine line between making too many decisions for our children and making too few. Making the distinction is the art of parenting. Be slow to judge other parents. If the right and wrong ways to raise kids were always obvious, all of us would do it correctly all the time.

Force-Feeding

A woman from Kansas remembers how, as a child, she was forced to eat everything on her plate. Living on a farm, her mother would pile food on her plate without regard for the child's individual taste or appetite. She was expected to clean her plate, and no excuse to the contrary was acceptable. Her mother would stand over her until every bite was eaten.

"Who's going to eat your food?" she would demand to know. "Uncle Pete isn't going to eat it. Grandfather is eating his food; he can't eat yours too. I guess you have to clean off your own plate."

An otherwise pleasant, loving mother turned into a drill sergeant at mealtime, barking orders. For someone visiting in the home the pressure was almost unbearable. To keep peace, the visitor felt obligated to make his own child eat all his food whether or not it was too much or the child didn't like something that was served.

Shouldn't the child have been allowed to choose the amount of food she had to eat? Couldn't she have been expected to sample varieties of food, but not forced to eat all of what she clearly did not like?

There's that fine line again. Find a healthy balance of foods your child absolutely needs and should eat and offer a variety of options.

The Seafood Allergy

Somewhere along the line, our son got the notion that seafood made him sick. It sounded like an excuse to me. I was certain he was faking it. Jim had a creative imagination and wasn't above using it to toy with his parents.

The real problem was that his father loved seafood and couldn't imagine any young lad turning it down.

After years of accepting his excuse, I decided to put my foot down. A plate of fish was planted firmly in front of Jim with the accompanying order to eat it, or else.

After much complaining, Jim took a few bites of the dreaded marine life. Almost immediately he began to turn red and get sick. I took the plate away and never asked him to eat fish again.

Children need to have some control at the dinner table. Often a child knows instinctively what he can't eat. It isn't a sin to let him make a few choices. Some parents seem to believe it to be a sign of rebellion if a child refuses any choice a parent makes.

Small Decisions Lead to Bigger Ones

If children aren't permitted to choose which shirt or blouse to wear or to pick out their own socks, how will they ever be able to make the big decisions later on?

How will they choose friends if they can't even select

a hairstyle? How will they pick activities to pursue if they aren't allowed to make any decisions about their own rooms?

We think we are protecting our kids from bad choices by keeping them from making any choices!

The biggest decision a child will ever make is regarding his relationship to Jesus Christ. And he must have a choice. That's the way God planned it. He will be better equipped to make the most important choice of all if he has had practice in decision-making on a smaller level.

"But if serving the Lord seems undesirable to you, then choose for yourselves this day whom you will serve. . . . But as for me and my household, we will serve the Lord" (Joshua 24:15).

We all know that our children must decide for themselves if they will be Christians. But we're prone to force that decision on them because it's so important to us.

Read the book of Ruth. Naomi, the loving mother-in-law, tries to make a decision for Ruth. She tells her to go back with her sister-in-law to her own people and her own gods. Naomi is certain she knows what's best for this young widow. Not afraid of making decisions, Ruth rejects Naomi's advice and stands up for what she believes. She will stay with Naomi.

"But Ruth replied, 'Don't urge me to leave you or to turn back from you. Where you go I will go, and where you stay I will stay. Your people will be my people and your God my God' " (Ruth 1:16).

Ruth wasn't afraid to exercise her God-given ability to make a decision. She felt confident she was choosing the right course, even if Naomi pressured her to do otherwise.

Moral Choices

When our daughter Mary reached her seventeenth birthday, she asked if she would now be allowed to attend R-rated movies. I told her the decision would have to be hers. Many parents won't agree with that much freedom, but I thought it was important.

Mary was too old to make a choice based on what she thought her father wanted her to do. Within a year she would be away at college in a large city, having to sift through all kinds of moral choices.

She must decide for herself, and I promised not to second-guess her. She didn't need a moral court or the shadow of a judgmental father hovering over her.

In reality, Mary could have done anything she wanted regardless of my permission. I'd have been foolish to try to control her as if she were on puppet strings.

Some readers won't remember when movies were such a big issue, but a couple of decades ago many Christians dared not admit that they even frequented movie theaters. The advent of home videos has now made this pretty much a non-issue in most places.

However, I do remember facing a crisis when Mary was still in early elementary school. I pastored a church at the time that had a number of members who believed movies were the devil's territory. One person believed that if you were in a movie theater when Christ returned, He wouldn't take you with Him. Convictions ran deep.

Mary came home from school one day asking if she could go to a Disney movie. To tell the truth, I winced inside. Our family went to shows whenever we traveled, but close to the steeple it was a touchy topic.

In my indecision the Lord seemed to speak to me. Questions like, "Whose child is this, anyway?" came to mind. And, "Who is responsible for her moral education, me or the church?" "When she has trials and difficulties, will the church be there to help, or will I have to handle the situation as her father?"

You guessed it. I told her she could go to the movie. Her father needed to show some moral authority. He couldn't cop out by letting others decide what was right or wrong for his child.

When I looked at that pretty young face, I knew I had to be a father who made choices based on what was best for her.

To the lasting credit of the church and its members, no one ever brought it up. They had their own principles but they proved loving and tolerant of others'.

Children need to observe their parents making difficult moral decisions. They also need to be encouraged to make those same choices for themselves.

9

I'd Smile More

Most young parents are fearful and for good reason. Responsibility for a new life is in their hands, and they feel frightfully insufficient for the task.

Fear steals a great deal of joy from parenting. I know it did for us. We had fun with our children, but there was always a certain amount of tension.

Are we feeding our baby the right foods? Are we burping him correctly? Will this new brand of diaper cause a rash? Are we overdressing or underdressing for the weather? Should we be crushing vitamins and slipping them into the strained peas?

What about school? Should we send her early because she loves to learn? Should we hold him back so he'll be one of the bigger kids in his class?

Here comes Santa Claus. Should we let the children believe in a mythical character who brings presents? What about the elf thing? Will it hurt them to learn about flying reindeer who prance around on chimneys?

With constant decisions like these to make, I'm afraid there weren't enough smiles. Parenting was more than serious business. It could be downright grim.

Uncertain, insecure, and inexperienced, we struggled to find our way as new parents. I'm sure there was a lot to smile about, but we took everything too seriously. Recently a friend of ours noticed the same thing. Looking through photos of our first child, he said, "Boy, you didn't smile much in those days."

The Lord gave us a thousand reasons to relax and be happy, but we didn't want to overdo it. We tried to show happiness at the proper times (everything was supposed to be proper); and we worked hard at avoiding spontaneity. After all, there was no telling what might result from unfettered joy and exuberance. A locked jaw set in concrete was much easier for young parents to master.

Then the grace of God moved in. I don't say this lightly. The grace of God isn't a term I toss around concerning every event in life. However, in this case I know my attitude was miraculously changed, and the sources of the change were not natural. The hand of God was definitely in it.

From Negative to Positive

Like millions of other parents, at first we saw parenting as a negative, hard-nosed, keep-the-lid-on-tight occupation. We didn't understand or trust positive reinforcement. Even to this day we sometimes get dirty looks when we suggest an encouraging approach.

Initially my motto was "Do what I say when I say it because I said it. If you don't do it, you are going to get it." Those two sentences sum up how I viewed parenting. I don't know where I got this philosophy. Was it from the movies or my parents or the church or school? I can't really say, but the attitude was deeply ingrained. Why would anyone, I thought, piddle around trying to motivate a child? What's to discuss? What's to talk about? Parents are dictators and children are subjects who ask "How high?" when we say "Jump."

One day for some reason God let me take a closer look, and I realized my children were terrified of me. They were getting barked at, and probably saw their dad as a military drill sergeant shouting orders. I knew there had to be a better, less intimidating way.

Nickel Sermons

At the time of this marvelous revelation, I was pastoring a wonderful country church. Each Sunday I mounted the platform and commanded that awesome pulpit while Pat sat in the pew with our three small children.

As I waxed eloquent our kids proceeded to tear their mother to shreds. They ran cars up her nose, tossed books on the floor, rolled pennies across the wooden pews, and tore at her nylons.

After each service I would come home exhilarated from speaking, only to find Pat nearly in tears, her hair pulled in all directions, clothes disheveled, arms scratched. I never had to ask, "How did the morning go?" Pat looked like a Chicago Bear linebacker after a Minnesota Vikings game (not quite, but I couldn't resist the comparison).

Being the bright person I am, I sensed that this couldn't go on. Super-dad came up with an idea. I commanded all three of the little terrorists to march into my office. Once there I explained the hard facts and our new policy.

"From now on," I said sternly, "if your mother says you were naughty in church, each of you gets spanked. Got that? *Everyone* gets spanked!" I roared, dismissing the tiny crew.

The next Sunday I came home shocked to find Pat collapsed in a heap. "All right!" I bellowed. "Everyone into the office." Smack, Wham, Thump. I did my parental duty and added a warning. "And don't let this happen again."

Seven days later Sunday rolled around and we went to church, came home, and spanked the kids. The following Sunday was the same routine. Church, home, spanking. We had established a new tradition. And everyone hated it.

Then the Lord gave me an idea. I called everyone into the office. They came dragging in, heads bent low. The office was no longer one of their favorite places.

"I have an idea," I began. "From now on everyone takes a piece of paper and a pencil to church. Each time I tell a story," (I told lots of stories) "you write a few words about it or draw a picture. For every story you write or draw something about, I'll pay you a nickel. Five stories gets a quarter. Ten stories, fifty cents."

When Sunday morning arrived we went to church and came home. This time Mother wasn't a basket case, and she didn't look like she had just returned from rag day at the mission.

The children followed me into the office and I counted stories. Each had a list complete with words (most misspelled) and drawings. There was a picture of a horse. I didn't remember a story about a horse, but if my child did, who was I to argue?

For seventy-five cents or a dollar we had peace at the Coleman home every Sunday after that. The children no longer hated church, I no longer played the bad guy, and Pat saved a fortune in hose.

Motivation

From then on we were believers in positive motivation. We still practiced the negative approach on occasion, but where we were previously all stick and no carrot, we added a lot more carrots.

This concept is still not accepted by many parents. We understand. It was a frightening change for us. Unfortunately, some parents go to an extreme of motivation by reward. A good balance is needed.

The book of Proverbs strikes a sensible medium.

"A gentle answer turns away wrath, but a harsh word stirs up anger" (15:1).

Grandparents understand the value of positive parenting. They aren't so likely to speak harshly to their grandchildren. In our advanced years we discover the strength in kind words and creative motivation.

"Pleasant words are a honeycomb, sweet to the soul and healing to the bones" (Proverbs 16:24).

Harsh Relationships

Some parents seem to *want* their children to grow up in a stern atmosphere. They see the heavenly Father as the "Great Frown in the Sky," and they don't want their children to forget it. There's no sense in arguing with someone who feels comfortable with an Uncomfortable God.

Only the grace of God is likely to change our minds and mend our ways. When we come to recognize and accept what the grace of God has accomplished in our lives, we'll be freed up to extend grace to our children. Unfortunately, if we see our relationship to God as a rigid, military-like business, we are likely to pass on the same outlook to our kids.

God's Face

During our days on earth we'll probably never see the face of God. But in the next life we expect to see our heavenly parent "face to face" (1 Corinthians 13:12). As Christians we're permitted to imagine all we want to about that face. How will God look? Not only His features, but how will His countenance appear? Is He the "Great Frown" or the "Wrinkled Brow" or the "Angry Eyes"? Or will we be greeted by the Loving Smile of Heaven?

When we know Him as the Loving Smile, we need to start early in showing that face to our children. It is through our sparkling eyes, our cavernous dimples, our rosy cheeks, and cheerful voice that our children will get a glimpse of God's friendly face.

I shouted at my children. I sternly warned them. I stared at them with my menacing glare. Did I also show the loving, accepting, and forgiving face that needs to go along with it?

Sometimes I did, but more often I didn't. Because God smiles at me, I hope I will share that smile with others as often as possible.

A Healthy Fear

Every child needs a healthy dose of parental respect. Parents can't be all smiles, all jolly, all tolerant, all positive all of the time. A child needs to know that his parent could and will come down tough, if necessary. That's because the Bible tells us not to neglect discipline.

Life is not a positive experience all of the time. Parents must withhold privileges, show disapproval, and deliver justice when the occasion warrants it.

The problem I found in the early years was that I was administering punishment as my sole source of control. I behaved as if the only way I could get anyone to move was with an electrical prod. The fact was that the prod was the only method I was willing to try. Indeed, it may have been the only method I knew.

The Wrong Approach

You will need to choose an effective approach to getting or keeping your child's school grades at an acceptable level. I chose to follow the negative method. Forgetting what I'd learned during those nickel-sermon days, I went right back to using sheer force in order to get their grades up to the level I expected.

If you've tried strict manipulation and it worked for you, congratulations. The experiment was less than successful for me and my clan.

Concerned that their grades were lower than they should be or could be, I developed a plan. If their grades were not as high as I expected, my children would have to spend time at physical labor. Each child had a turn at digging in the garden, raking leaves, or stacking wood.

I gave them ample warning that their next report card would determine how long they toiled at these menial tasks.

Report card day came and I struck my best Simon Legree pose. After poring over their grades, I announced my sentences and condemned each child to their allotted time of work. Satisfied that I had completed my parental duty, I warned them that the consequences could be even more dire after the next grading period.

Nine weeks later, I was ranting and raving over their new report cards and sending them back to the school of hard labor.

Looking back now, I know what I accomplished—absolutely nothing. If I'd done nothing to try to improve their grades, the result would have been exactly the same. By their own standards, at their own speed, they were deciding how important grades were to them. They weighed the options and asked themselves what price they were willing to pay. I'm convinced, nothing their parents did to try to control their choices had any effect.

The most important thing parents can do is to open doors so their children can become what they want to be. And, hopefully, to pave the way for what God wants to bring about in their lives. Permission, affirmation, and encouragement are far better motivators than control.

A Cheerful Look

It won't hurt a child to receive an occasional frown or harsh look from those in authority. Raising kids can't be a daily trip to Pleasureville. But children deeply need the cheerful look. The look that says, "Let's find a happy solution to this." A child who grows up looking into a cheerful face is more likely to develop a smiling face of her own.

The author of Proverbs put it this way: "A cheerful look brings joy to the heart" (15:30).

Joy is contagious. Children pick it up from their parents as surely as they develop the same accent, tastes in food, or love of a baseball team. Joyfulness seeps through the cracks and overwhelms a child in the most pleasant way.

Every child deserves to see at least one smiling face on a daily basis. A child is especially blessed if he gets to look up into two smiling faces every day at home.

10

The Relative Connection

Relatives are a mixed bag. We like to speak well of our brothers, sisters, and cousins, but not all of us have great stories to tell. Some may have an uncle in Spokane whom they hope their children never meet. Not everyone has a neat little package of clan members they can boast about. Even grandmothers or grandfathers might be candidates for this week's most-wanted list.

That's the unfortunate reality. But wherever we do have courageous, loving, or even tolerable relatives, our child needs to know about them.

Take our Grandmother Tingle from Pittsville, Maryland, for instance. As a young lady she became a widow, with four children to raise. Battling against all odds, Grandmother Tingle worked hard to hold a small farm together during the most difficult of times. Her children started jobs at early ages, ran a local store, went to college, taught school, and made something of themselves.

Eventually the Tingle children became our children's

grandmother, great aunt, and great uncles. They helped form the heritage of our three children.

Our relatives didn't lead the charge at Gettysburg, or become President of the United States. They were and are people of character who braved the storms of life, fought in wars, declared their faith in God, and lent a generous hand to their fellow human beings.

Today's Mobility Separates Families

Every grown child should be free to make a life for himself. He must interpret and accept God's leading as he sees it.

No child should sit around chained to his family of origin. Each must sail the oceans, climb the mountains, and walk along the beaches of his dreams. Smart parents cut their children loose and bid them God-speed.

Unfortunately, the gift of mobility is also a curse.

For instance, I have a wonderful eighty-seven-year-old aunt, Mildred, living in Hanover, Pennsylvania. We wish our children had gotten to know her better when they were young. But in our mobile world that wasn't easy.

I grew up in a splintered, dysfunctional family with hardly any family ties. After finishing seminary, Pat and I forged west to follow the Lord's leading.

One result of our westward move is that we have had little contact with Aunt Mildred. Our children know her less. That's a loss for all of us. We don't regret where we went or what we did. We simply wish we had kept in closer contact. We'd have benefited greatly from Aunt Mildred's love for the Lord, and our children would have tasted the flavor of their distinctive roots.

There are books written on how to keep in contact across the miles, if you need ideas. One family tended a garden at their grandmother's house so they could have a built-in reason to visit once a week. Another grandma lived far away from her children and grandchildren, but they kept in touch by mail, telephone, and regular visits.

It may be helpful to make a schedule for visits. It needs to be a priority and put on the calendar, whether it's once a week, once a month, once every six months, or a year. Avoid excuses such as being too busy, it's too much effort, you can't afford it, or even that you don't think the relatives want to see you (unless you know that to be true). Plan trips to be enjoyable, on the way and when you get there. Make stops at interesting places, take pictures, and keep a journal of your activities. Ask your relatives to take you to places of interest in their town. Most would love to show you around.

You can't place a value on a friendship that is allowed to develop between a child and his grandparent or between him and an uncle or aunt. A child's life is fuller if he has the opportunity to make friends with his relatives. Together they can build warm memories that last throughout their lives.

If we had it to do over again, we would stop more often at the refreshing homes of our relatives and invite them more to ours.

Faith of Our Fathers and Mothers

Our daughter Mary had to ask us what her Grandfather Marshall was like, because he died before our kids were born. His absence left a void in their lives.

We were happy to tell her what a wonderful person he was. She would have loved him and he would have cherished her.

Connection with extended family is significant. Our past has enough blank pages. It even has several black holes. Whenever possible, we need to fill in the blanks with cheerful memories of the people who count most in our lives—family.

Proverbs tells us of a father connecting with his child. He tells his boy what it was like living in his own father's house.

"When I was a boy in my father's house, still tender, and an only child of my mother, he taught me and said, 'Lay hold of my words with all your heart; keep my commands and you will live' " (4:3–4).

Biblical writers made lots of significant family connections. That's one of the reasons why the Bible was written. The authors wanted to make sure their children remembered the faith of their fathers. The stories are true to life—not sanitized, but extremely honest—and these accounts enable us to connect with our genealogical and spiritual parents.

Connect While They're Young

Two major mistakes we tend to make with regard to relatives is waiting until our children are too old to benefit significantly from their experience and influence, and, secondly, erroneously using family stories to control our children.

I wish we'd told our children more about their family "connections" when they would have enjoyed them; they loved stories when they were preschoolers. Teenagers by and large don't want to hear those stories; they are too wrapped up in their own lives to want to hear many family tales. Someday down the road they will probably want to hear about their roots, hopefully not so far down the road that there is no one left to share them.

In our book *Eight Things Not to Say to Your Teen,** we discuss storytelling at some length. Stories about relatives should be told in a relaxed atmosphere without a hard edge or hidden agenda. They need to be shared in an open, friendly environment and told for sheer enjoyment. Then when an appropriate situation arises, children will be able to apply the stories to their own lives.

Building a Dam

Tom Brokaw, NBC News anchorman, tells the story of his working-class family and their move to South Dakota. His father took a job building a huge dam near Yankton. So many people moved there for the construction job that a new town was created to accommodate them.

In his fifties now, Brokaw beamed with pride as he told the story. As he said, this was a wonderful era. Parents like his pulled themselves out of the Depression, won a World War, and tackled huge modern projects. Their sons, like Tom, made their way through college and took their piece of the American pie.

Even if our children reject family stories for a while, they'll eventually learn to appreciate them. Only recently have I become proud of a grandfather I hardly knew who worked in a stone quarry in northern Maryland. But today I feel connected to him and to my uncles who labored daily at demanding jobs.

Just last year I drove back to the area where my other grandfather lived. Though I never met the man, I enjoyed looking down the road that was named after him. I tried to imagine what kind of farmer-businessman he must have been. I wish I knew more about him, but that is not always possible.

---

*Bethany House Publishers, 1994.

Relatives Are Not Always a Source of Pride

What do you do when you have a relative who has proven to be harmful to society? Your children should obviously be protected from those who have been guilty of abuse, drunkenness, theft, or wreckless endangerment.

I'm not talking about an obnoxious uncle or a cousin who tells boring stories. Occasionally a relative is more than a social misfit; he can be dangerous.

It may be difficult or painful to keep children away from their own flesh and blood, but it may be necessary, for a time, for their own safety.

It's Not Worth a Guilt Trip

Don't put a guilt trip on your grown kids if they don't wish to keep in touch with relatives.

Author James Dickey said he grew up in an era when it was immoral not to know your cousins. That must have been a wonderful time and place. Would that all of us could have been brought up in such an atmosphere. But most of us were not. And it is not always possible to maintain the paradise of the extended family over the years.

Now that our children have grown, we don't try to manipulate them into keeping in touch with family. They must decide who they will be close to or who they can practically visit on a regular basis. Adult children don't need or appreciate parents who are always attempting to arrange get-togethers for them with relatives.

The time to have these gatherings, in which family can become acquainted, and even become friends, is when the children are young and don't have so many outside activities. Then, when they are grown, there might be a natural bond that will be ongoing.

We can only pray that our children will find some degree of connection with their relatives. As adults they will have to work this out in their own way.

11

Soothe the Savage

William Congreve authored this accurate bit of wisdom:

Music hath charms to soothe the savage breast,
To soften rocks or bend a knotted oak.
                    —"The Mourning Bride"

Most families could benefit from this method of soothing the savage breast. Are we browbeating or soothing the "savage" in adolescence? If music can contribute even minimally to the reduction of primal hostilities, it is well worth the effort.

The right kind of music at the appropriate time helps to adjust attitudes and mediate the atmosphere in a home. Many of us have experienced music's power to charm, and wish we had experimented with it more in our early years of parenting.

No one doubts the power rooted in the music frequently played by teenagers. The sheer volume and beat is enough to send entire households rushing to their battle stations. Parents, children, teens, and even grandparents are soon protecting themselves and hurling verbal missiles at the offending noise.

"Do you have to play that so loud?"

"Why can't you put on a nature tape?"

"That kid's going to burst an eardrum!"

"Has anyone seen my Perry Como Christmas album?"

"That's the same kind of beat savages use."

"It's the devil's music."

If music has the potential to disrupt the family, surely it must have the necessary properties to calm, soothe, and relax.

At least it would be worth trying to find out.

It's Not Always in the Genes

It would be safe to say that music wasn't a top priority in our home. In spite of this, June excelled at piano and Mary competed in state competitions with her trombone.

But I wish music had been a bigger part of our lives. The warm scenes of a family singing around the piano would have been a wonderful memory. Apart from family enrichment and just plain fun, singing and playing songs together would certainly have had spiritual (and physical) benefits. Not that we would have sung together at community gatherings in matching outfits. That isn't for everyone and I *know* it wouldn't have been for us.

Music as Worship

When you feel great gratitude toward a loving God, you may wish you could express yourself musically. I often feel this vacuum in my life. Whether it's joy and thankfulness or sadness and despair, music is an excellent outlet for deep emotions. Some days words just aren't enough. Sometimes cries of anguish or even shouts of joy fall short. The Bible is packed with admonitions to vent our emotions through musical instruments.

Unfortunately, music is closely identified with performing. But worship doesn't have to be a professional production. I love to hear a shaky trumpet player who gives it all he's got to express his thanks to God.

Unlimited Opportunities

By the time this book goes to print our current musical opportunities could well be outdated. The industry is changing and advancing so rapidly that today's audio system is tomorrow's antique. It's a short trip from the music store to the museum.

Nevertheless, a few simple instruments remain and are quite capable of adjusting the mind and soul. A guitar strummed in the most elementary style is still as meaningful as the stringed instruments played by shepherd boys in the far-off hills of Israel.

I tried to get members of my family to take up the guitar. It was the same old story: frustrated father tries to push his dream off on his kids. But it was my personal dream, and no one else picked it up.

The other day Pat got out our old record player. It's the same one we used to serenade our children. This time she got it out to amuse Nolan, our six-month-old grandson.

Soon he was cooing and smiling to the same records his mother, Mary, heard a generation ago. Among them was Mr. Rogers singing about how special each child is and how much he means in the lives of others. No doubt Nolan will listen to these records many more times, and hopefully they will add to his sense of security and belonging.

Ideally, music will contribute something positive to the atmosphere. Atmosphere in a home is extremely significant in the lives of little children getting acquainted with their surroundings.

More musical possibilities are coming. Our computers now have the capacity to sing and play like a CD player. Instruments are available on which nearly anyone can play recognizable tunes within minutes. Even the tonally-challenged (such as myself) can participate in musical expression that previously would have been unthinkable.

Spiritual Benefits of Music

In our search for materials and resources to enrich our children's souls and spirits, we too often ignore the obvious. Music is a great help in our quest for godly awareness in our children.

"Speak to one another with psalms, hymns and spiritual songs. Sing and make music in your heart to the Lord" (Ephesians 5:19).

We did enjoy singing before meals when our children were small; a short chorus of thanksgiving seemed like the right touch from time to time. We still do it when our adult family gathers, and the blending of their voices is music to my ears.

The psalmist expressed himself musically when he overflowed with thanksgiving to God: "Let us come before him with thanksgiving and extol him with music and song" (95:2).

New Music

Home is also the ideal place to introduce new music. Let it become the ground where new sounds and new lyrics are heard and shared with one another.

Children often have difficulty identifying with the old hymns and anthems of the organized church. Let your children choose the music they enjoy and can relate to.

A delightful tape that came my way in recent years was a sing-along Christian worship service. The leader introduced each song and then encouraged participation of the listeners. The songs were easy to learn, contemporary, uplifting, and filled with praise to the Lord.

Parents don't have to be great musicians themselves or take courses in music appreciation. The equipment, devices, and instruments are plentiful and growing every day. Children of all ages can benefit from the enrichment music brings into the home.

12

Pitch a Tent

One of the best investments we ever made was in a 10' x 16' Sears & Roebuck tent. A huge canvas monster with aluminum poles and a floor, this contraption became a member of our family. Like a stray cat, it showed up one day and never left.

We stuffed that old home-away-from-home in the trunk of many a car and drove to countless exciting destinations across the United States and Canada. We also set it up many times in our backyard so the kids could sleep out under the stars.

Years ago the University of Nebraska did some studies on strong families. Among their findings they learned that a large number of strong families were campers. There are unlimited benefits that come from sleeping on the ground, smacking mosquitoes, and eating sand-covered food—together.

I didn't grow up camping; none of it comes naturally to me. And yet some of my most pleasant memories center around a campfire with our children, or gazing up at the moon and stars at midnight in an open field.

The Accordion Effect

When families go camping, the rules change. Every home has its household rules: Don't put your feet on the couch; take your dishes to the sink; be in bed by nine; put your dirty clothes in the hamper, and on it goes. Everyone gets tired of those rules, no matter how necessary they may be.

Camping allows a family to forget the house rules for a few days. Wilderness living has few regulations and many rewards: Don't play with snakes that rattle; put on the mosquito repellent; take your turn at gathering wood; showers and washing behind your ears are optional; and there's no bedroom to pick up, dishes to wash, or homework to do.

During the day the family does some things together and then splits up in different directions. You return for a meal and take off again. (That's the accordion effect.) Family members pair off in assorted combinations: father/daughter, father/son, brother/sister, mother/daughter, father/mother, etc.

One parent told us how their family created the same relaxed atmosphere when traveling on business. She and her husband made it a point of taking their sons along whenever possible. Their accommodations were hotels and motels, but the principle was much the same as camping. The four visited theaters, historical sites, museums, and local centers of interest. The parents and children gained experience and knowledge and quality time together, while taking a break from the rules and routine of home.

Tents, pull-out campers, and RVs are not the only essential ingredients to family time away—they are merely common ones.

Without a doubt, enjoying changes of scenery and location become some of our children's best memories.

And generally it turns out to be quite pleasant for Mom and Dad too.

Most of us can remember sliding down a slippery bank into a creek or falling into the lake from an upset canoe. You can't make memories like that watching *The Purple Blob That Swallowed Seattle* on TV.

The Spaghetti Shower

Our family camped in many different combinations. Sometimes all five of us went together. Frequently I took one or two of the children. Often just Jim and I went.

One of my most vivid memories was when Jim spilled his box of BBs on the forest floor. Being a frugal lad, he insisted on picking up each one. Super-dad couldn't abandon his young son to the horrific job, so he hunched down to help. *What bonding,* I thought.

The next day I suffered a raging red rash contracted from poison ivy, poison oak, or poison something. For weeks I battled an insane itching on both hands and arms. Naturally, Jim didn't raise one mark over the stuff.

On another occasion when our whole family went camping, Jim and I begged Pat to let us cook a meal. After all, we had honed our culinary skills on many an open fire in the woods. (Camping changed somewhat when Mother came along. She thought washed hands were still a must, as well as clean food, and keeping cupcake intake to a minimum. She didn't seem to appreciate the wilderness-type camping as much as Jim and I did.)

Pat consented.

We took a can of spaghetti out of the trunk and placed it over the heated coals. That was the way Jim and I were used to cooking. No fuss. No muss.

Soon we wandered off, leaving our can of supper to simmer to perfection.

Minutes later, innocent, unsuspecting June came strolling by the fire.

Suddenly, without warning . . . K A-B O O O M!

The *unopened* can exploded, sending tiny, wet spaghetti rings shooting tree-high into the air. June stood petrified as the heavens rained down the gooey mess.

Spaghetti sauce covered our car and our tent. The sticky rings clung to June's hair like paste.

Our daughter was silent as she washed her hair. I'm not sure how long it was before she was able to speak. But if you ask her about her camping memories today, don't be surprised if a tear comes to her eye.

Short- and Long-Term Benefits

The best rewards of camping come while you're experiencing it. That weekend. That day. That moment. Camping isn't like flute lessons, where years later you realize how beneficial they were. Families smell the campfire, eat the burnt marshmallows, enjoy walks in the woods, and run from the slithering snake right in the here and now.

From these immediate gratifications are born memories that give everyone a warm sense of belonging to the people they shared camp with. For decades afterward, you'll sit around and tell stories about the night the tornado hit or the evening the floods swamped the tent and everyone ran for the car. You'll reminisce about telling stories with the lights out, listening to ball games over a staticky radio, and stumbling around in the dark looking for an outhouse, hoping you don't have to share it with another mammal.

Maybe our children won't share our appreciation for camping when they grow up. But at least the quiet of an early morning and the smell of breakfast cooking over an open fire won't be totally foreign to them.

Jesus Pitched His Tent

There is a passage of Scripture that means more to me because of our camping experiences. Whenever I read it, this verse stands up on the page and waves a flag.

John 1:14, TLB, says this: "Christ became a human being and lived here on earth among us."

The phrase "lived here on earth among us" could be translated "pitched His tent among us."

I know this doesn't mean that Christ went camping near Mormon Island and stuck His feet in the Platte River. The tents the nomads lived in back then were more like homes.

And yet I choose to claim the verse for myself because it's a reminder to me that Christ is never far away. When we pitched our tent on the sand near the river, with thorns grabbing our sneakers, Jesus was there and He pitched His tent among us.

13

Build Self-Confidence

When our children had reached the ages of fourteen, twelve, and ten we began some of our great experiments in young-adult independence. We wanted them to handle more of their own decision-making, so we gave them plenty of extra rope (hopefully not enough to make a noose).

For one thing, Pat and I decided it was time the children learned to take care of their own clothes beyond hanging them in the closet or keeping them in a drawer. From then on, they would be expected to wash, dry, and iron them as well. In our home, with modern equipment, this could hardly be considered slave labor.

Our ultimate goal was that in allowing our children to make some of their own decisions they would become more responsible. No longer did we hear a child whine, "Where is my blue blouse?" or, "Could you get my new jeans ready for tomorrow?" Those questions were already answered. The blue blouse was wherever you left it. The new jeans would be ready tomorrow if you got them ready.

Being responsible for their own clothes dissolved a lot of hassling and bickering. There now existed a short straight line between what a child needed and the fulfillment of that need. A shirt needed was a shirt washed and ironed by the person who needed it.

Not that there weren't exceptions. Emergencies, surprises, and unexpected changes in plans called for help from a loving parent or even a caring sibling. But normally there was no doubt as to who would care for a shirt, blouse, or pair of pants—the owner would.

None of this came about or was demanded out of anger or rancor. We weren't trying to play drill sergeant or see how bossy we could be. It was simply a practical solution. Why should the children sit around watching television while their mother did the entire wash and ironing? Self-sufficiency was too valuable a lesson to miss out on.

Many mothers tell horror stories of their children returning home from college for the weekend or for a holiday—bearing sacks of dirty clothes for Mom to wash and iron.

Parents with self-sufficient children don't have this complaint. College students are more than capable of caring for their own clothes. They're welcome to save a few bucks and enjoy the convenience of their parents' washer and dryer, but they don't need a day-maid to iron their ruffles or press their pleats.

The wisdom of the ages is to be found in the book of Proverbs. It warns about people who don't learn to prepare their own things: "The lazy man does not roast his game, but the diligent man prizes·his possessions" (12:27).

Every child will benefit from learning to "roast his own game." It's much harder to learn this the first week of college or, worse yet, the first week of marriage.

Teaching kids the particular responsibility of washing their own clothes works well because it takes no threatening on the part of parents to see it accomplished. While dishwashing takes perseverance and reinforcement, no child wants to wake up on a school morning without the "right" thing to wear. This personal exercise has its own built-in discipline.

There's Nothing to Do!

How do you react when a child groans, "I'm bored. There's nothing to do"? Some parents take it personally. They consider themselves the family recreation director and snap to it, looking for some way to entertain this poor child.

There are some basics everyone must learn:
1. I am responsible for my own happiness.
2. I am responsible for my own possessions.
3. I am responsible for my own time.
4. I am responsible for my own success.
5. I am responsible for my own health.
6. I am responsible for my own mental state.
7. I am responsible for my own spirituality.
8. I am responsible for my own habits.
9. I am responsible for my own self-esteem.
10. I am responsible for my own attitude.
11. I am responsible for my choice of friends.

From early childhood, we either learn to accept these responsibilities as our own or we behave as though someone else is at fault when things don't go right. Every person must learn to accept the vital role he plays in shaping and maintaining his own life.

The "I Can't Help It" Generation

Parent: "Why haven't you finished your homework?"
Child: "I can't help it that the teacher gave me too much to do!"

Parent: "Have you found my tape recorder yet?"

Child: "My friend borrowed it from me. I can't help it that he hasn't returned it."

Parent: "Why haven't you finished the dishes?"

Child: "I can't help it that I needed to call my friend back before I could finish."

By accepting these responses as valid, a parent helps create a victim mentality in the child. And while such an attitude has an adverse effect on a child, it can cripple an adult.

If I can't find my shoes, I have a problem. I will not have them to wear when I need them unless I find them myself. That is the reality of self-sufficiency.

Little boys who rely on their mothers to find their shoes grow up to be husbands who expect their wives to find their shoes. As children, their parents allow them to be completely dependent. Later in life they look for adults who will keep that pattern going for them.

Of course, a mother who dotes too much on her child doesn't automatically create a dependent adult. A grown child can still choose for himself to be self-sufficient, but it will be more difficult for him if he has not had some training in it while young.

Parents show the most wisdom and love when they guide their children toward reasonable self-sufficiency. Coupled with reasonable care, this gives a child the tools to decide what kind of adult he will be. You may ask, "What is reasonable?" As we have said before, parenting is an art. None of us can decide for someone else what is reasonable for their children.

Picking Up After Them

When our children were small we were terribly concerned about a neat house. After they finished playing with something, we wanted them to pick up their toys like perfect children do. In our enthusiasm to maintain a neat house and orderly children, we helped them collect their dolls, cars, balls, and puzzles and put them into the toy box.

Most of the time, what we really did was talk a great deal about how they had to pick up their toys. While we talked, pleaded, cajoled, *we* ended up putting away the toys.

"We aren't going anywhere until these are picked up!" was the threat we made while we scooped the toys into the box. The greater our threat, the faster we tossed the toys into their proper slots. If we were totally fed up and frustrated, we could clean up that mess in record time!

Our children soon understood the system far better than we did. If Dad was terribly upset, he would have the toys picked up before the kids could move in that direction. Especially if he began with the warning: "Now, I'm not going to pick up these toys! The one who got them out is going to pick them up."

That relentless edict simply meant Dad was in a bigger hurry than usual. The children must have watched in amusement and amazement at how the adult mind worked.

Up, Up, and Away

Sometime during that magical era of lessons on independence and self-sufficiency, we were persuaded that our children were old enough to go on an airplane by themselves. We told them that if they paid for the airline tickets (we were broke) they could fly back to see their grandparents, aunts, uncles, and cousins all by themselves.

Mary looked at me and said, "Wow! We'll get treated real special, won't we?" (Evidently she wasn't being treated special where she lived!)

A friend who worked for the airlines told us how carefully they'd be looked after from one airport to the other. He assured us they'd be safer than anyone else on the plane. When they transferred at O'Hare in Chicago, our young urchins would be handled like rare cargo.

We decided to go for it. The kids began working at odd jobs: delivering newspapers, baby-sitting, returning bottles for cash, and stashing away their allowances. Soon they had proudly mustered up their designated amounts.

On the day of their departure, we took them to the airport and watched them walk the gangplank to board the plane. Our hearts swelled at the adventure of it all. When I was their age I'd only traveled by car to one other city.

Our kids were off to see the world without a parent anywhere in sight. Pat and I, proudly satisfied, returned to our village near the Platte River and waited to hear of their safe arrival.

A week later we reported back to the same airport ready to collect our weary travelers. Nature has no beauty to compare with the sight of our children's faces when they bounded off that plane. We were ecstatic and grateful to the Lord to see our cheerful trio home safely.

As we stood by the baggage area waiting for their luggage, I whispered, "See that man standing by the wall? That's Governor Exon. He must have been on your plane. Somebody should go over and say hello to him."

Ten-year-old June perked up at the exciting prospect. Without hesitation, she walked over to the tall gentleman and extended her hand.

"Hi, my name is June Coleman. I'm in the fifth grade in Aurora."

The two shook hands and exchanged pleasantries. For all we know they could have shared state secrets.

Experiences like that build confidence in children. It was June's choice, and she got the thrill of meeting the governor while the rest of us stood there like a flock of frozen geese.

When I think back on it, there are so many things we could have done to encourage our children to spread their wings and test the heights.

Every child needs to know they *can* do things on their own, and they can't learn it by standing on the sidelines. They need to test their abilities and see how self-sufficient they can become.

Self-Confidence Is Not a Contradiction

Some parents are afraid of self-confidence because it sounds self-centered, even egotistical. They want their children to grow up with confidence in the Lord, not in themselves. Parents need to know that self-confidence and confidence in God are not in competition with each other.

The correct balance rests in that fantastic passage in the book of Philippians: "Being confident of this, that he who began a good work in you will carry it on to completion until the day of Christ Jesus" (1:6).

Confident that God has given us ability.

Confident that God will help us use that ability.

Confident that God continues to add to our ability.

Confident that God is doing a good work in us.

Confident that God will keep increasing our ability until Christ returns.

No one can give a child greater confidence than that.

14

Ride the Screaming Plunger

There are certain ages when children are more likely to want to do things with their parents. Part of skillful parenting is knowing when to do things with a child and when to back off. Very young children can hardly wait to frolic in the park, proud to be with their dad or mom. But usually teenagers don't like to be seen with their parents, who to them can be embarrassing (they look old or oddly dressed).

The key is to recognize the windows of opportunity at the early ages and seize them. Sadly, we're often chasing other rainbows when the skies around home are the best.

We used to do things together as a family in one of two ways. We would take the children somewhere to watch them play or perform, or we'd actually do things together with them. Both kinds of activities are important. The second kind, where we played, worked, or explored together is by far the most lasting in our memories and probably had the most significant influence on our kids.

Amusement parks and playgrounds are places children will want to experience sooner or later. But parents can't always participate in everything their child does there. You may have noticed how parents tend to sit on benches, holding jackets and backpacks, waiting for the rides to end.

We took our children to many amusement parks. When we could or when we dared we went on the rides with them. This was no small feat. We found it hard to ride the Screaming Plunger, dropping seventy feet in half a second, and still look courageous to the youngsters. But we tried.

I vividly recall one incident when our children begged us incessantly to try out a particular death-defying machine. Pat refused; she decided holding coats had to be done by someone and she volunteered to sacrifice.

The three children ended up going on the Ride of No Return (or something like that) by themselves. As they staggered down the ramp afterward, Pat walked over to greet them.

"Oh, Mom!" June exclaimed. "You've got to go on this ride."

No sooner had she spoken the words when she threw up all over her mother's shoes. Needless to say, Pat declined the offer to try the ride.

Some events may be off-limits for parents, but the most memorable family outings are those in which everyone participates. Standing and watching has its place; joining in and getting wet and dirty is better.

Learning With the Animals

Even the most sedate personality will enjoy watching animals frolic together. Not just animal siblings, but parents playing with their baby critters is a common sight in the wild or even in zoos.

There may be some serious survival training taking place, but the main objective may be simply to have fun.

River otters are the most obvious examples of a carefree family having quality time together. Monkeys especially enjoy teasing and vigorously chasing one another. Foxes learn togetherness playing in the bushes, along with a few basic hunting skills.

Creative playtime is a good learning time for children as well. They learn how to give and take, win and lose, and get a bump or bruise now and then without serious consequences. They also learn the problems created when they go off and pout or refuse to follow the rules.

Lion prides spend hours roughhousing and rolling in the grass. Polar bears like to chase each other in the snow, tumble over the frozen tundra, and swim underwater.

The psalmist tells us that God made the huge sea creatures to play in the open waters:

"There the ships go to and fro and the leviathan, which you formed to frolic there" (104:26).

Animals have much to teach us. One thing is the obvious importance they place on playtime.

Relax the Control

Ever since our children were little we've played football in one of the nearby parks. Last week we played another game—only now all of them are in their twenties.

Eager to get a game going, I've never been one to stand around while the group makes up the rules. It has always been painful for me to wait while others sort out how we will proceed. All I want to do is play ball or get hopping with whatever it is we are going to do, so consequently I usually call the shots, at least with my family.

"It's two-hand touch, four plays is all you get, the big tree is the goal line, and the pine trees are out of bounds." Simple, huh? No one ever played football by committee. Let's get moving!

It used to bother the kids that I always made the rules. It probably still does. I just think a game as monumental as football calls for leadership. I don't want to spend more time talking about the game than playing it.

But I'm trying to limit my control these days. After the rules are announced, everyone takes turns being quarterback or whatever position they want. We play hard but no one cares who wins. We spend little time arguing over what's fair or foul. We enjoy the exercise and the company. Today our grown children are the ones who suggest we play. In a few years I hope to see my grandchildren call plays in those same familiar parks.

Stubborn old Grandpa will probably still be barking out, "All right, it's two-hand touch, four plays is all you get. . . ."

But in order for play to be *play*, we have to stop being control freaks. Normally, play should be mutual and cooperative. Parents have to create a level playing field whenever possible. Adults will have to insist that children not play in the street, or say when it's time to come in for supper, but in most areas we need to strive for reciprocity.

That means adult and child both get on the ground

and get their knees wet. Everyone gets the same number of trucks and cars or whatever and a comparable amount of sand in their shoes. Parents who stand above their children and watch them play live in a different world.

Worlds meld together on sandy riverbanks, on the family room floor, and out on the limb of a sturdy oak tree.

Adults who play "me boss" miss out on the fun of playing video games and shooting water pistols *with* their kids.

Play for the Sheer Sake of Togetherness

Like most parents, we wanted our children to be bright and learn quickly. When our oldest daughter was still a preschooler we bought her a microscope. I pictured her identifying amoeba and bacteria before she went to kindergarten.

Fortunately, Mary was rescued by her father's inability to make the microscope work. I didn't have the patience to put molds in the fridge and cultivate a tiny fungus between two pieces of glass.

Soon Mary and I went back to where we belonged. We learned to play for the moment. We played until we laughed. We played for the simple joy of it. We didn't have a program or schedule, so we could get the most out of goofing off.

Never again would I make our time together part of a gigantic educational scheme. Have a tea party for the sake of pretending and being together. Create a play and dress up for the sheer fun of it.

A veteran schoolteacher told me this story: At a parent/teacher conference a mother told her, "I'm doing my best to correct my daughter's English. Daily we go round and round over her abuse of grammar. It's really become a strain in our home, but I wanted you to know I'm trying."

The wise teacher responded, "Why don't you back off? It isn't worth the hassle. Spend more time playing with her and I'll take care of the double negatives."

The key is to play for the fun of it, to get down to their level, to identify with their experience. The goal is to make the best of the time we have with our children while they still want to be around us. If other benefits are gained, so be it.

If I Could Play Again

Don't waste your time trying to turn back the clock. It can't be done. But if somehow a time machine could send us back to play with our children again, here's what I'd do differently:

- I'd be available for more hairdos. Daughters love to play beauty shop with their father's thinning hair. I'd let them put more goop in it, comb it any way they want, and watch them laugh.
- I'd spend more time giving horsey rides on the living room floor. I miss the days when all three kids would climb on my back and I'd prance around and gyrate until they fell off. I'd give almost anything to hear their squeals of laughter again.
- I'd watch more homegrown dramas. It was always painful to stop watching a football game to go to the basement to see the children perform a play for us. What a fool I was. What I wouldn't give now to leave a game and see their pride and excitement as they acted out their own creative productions just for us.

- I'd love to stand again at almost any event and let the kids take turns sitting on my shoulders so they could see—Thanksgiving Day parades, zoos, political speeches, migrating birds, and baseball games. Surely that's why God gave parents shoulders. Shoulders are the honored seats where children sit so they can see the world.
- I'd spend less time on the beach and more time in the water. Those shoulders also make great diving boards for little guys and gals.
- I'd read more books to them—even the ones we'd read a dozen times or more. You know, the stories they've heard so often they correct you if you change one word.
- I'd go camping more often. I'd toss Frisbees in the fields, walk along the riverbanks with them, gather wood, roast marshmallows, and tell them ghost stories. I'd look for lost watches, BBs, and pocketknives in the tall grass.
- I'd do more hands-on activities. I'd take up more hobbies that we could pursue together—play more tennis, miniature golf, and softball on Saturday or Sunday afternoons.
- Tea parties were always hard for this dad to endure. I wish I could try that again. I'd make a bigger fuss over their place settings and dainty dishes. I'd eat each cracker with relish and sip my "tea" more leisurely. And I'd ask for seconds—maybe thirds.

Looking back, it's easier to see where the true treasures of life lie. They're buried in sandboxes. Packed inside water pistols. Scattered across football fields and baseball diamonds. Drifting along the shallow bottom of the Platte River. Crawling on the shores of the Chesapeake Bay. Dotted on the winding trails of the Rocky Mountains.

Hard work has its own reward but so does fun. The best pictures in our family albums weren't taken in posed positions in photographer's studios. They're the snapshots of kids and teenagers smiling and laughing in the kitchen or the backyard.

Children know the value of play. Adults often lose their concept of it and turn it into exercise. That's why people dedicated to exercise look so serious and somber. They may be active, but unfortunately they're also drowning in their goals and programs. Children have fun while remaining oblivious to the benefits. Consequently, the benefits flow as natural perks that come from enjoying themselves.

Hopefully, your children will be able to call you back to your senses. They want you to leave the computer (or teach them how to play games on it), turn off the lamp at your desk, and go out sledding with them. Because adults don't think sledding is "productive" they tend to degrade such activities. Children are too preoccupied with the fun of playing to take time to analyze the productivity level.

It's better to let your children have their own way more often in this area and dislodge you from the tense cocoons where you frequently hide. Blessed are the parents who have children who teach them to play again.

Dr. Paul Welter tells us that some productive-oriented parents need to do some kind of craft before they can let themselves play.* If you are an adult who must produce something, enjoying play for the sake of play alone will be hard for you. But making a wall plaque, a

---

Counseling and the Search for Meaning (Word Publishers, 1987), p. 192.

potholder, a bookend, or a doll's dress with your child builds a bridge too.

There are two areas where parental attitudes toward play could be improved:

First, allow your children to play more often. Don't try to structure it. Don't discourage it.

And second, play *with* them.

15

Set Unusual Goals

Every time I see a certain ad on television I wince. It's the one where a determined mother says, "I think every parent would like to see their child become a doctor."

Is that really true? Do all children fall into one of two categories: those who become doctors (the winners) and those who become anything else (the losers)? Are we saying that receptionists may be all right, but radiologists are somehow better?

Has our society degenerated to the place where people with certain occupations are considered of higher value than those with blue-collar jobs?

What Are the Important Goals?

We never sat down and wrote out a list of goals for our children. Neither of us believed that was important or necessary. But if I had it to do over again, I would make a conscientious, thoughtful list of what I'd like to see each of them accomplish in their three score or more years.

However, the list would *not* include the name of an educational institution or a career of any kind. I believe those goals and ambitions are up to the individual child, not the parents.

I am a professional. I have a master's degree and have been known to give advice to others now and then. But frequently I have wondered what it would be like to be a laborer of some kind. Many professionals, especially women, have said they would like to be home with their children more than they are able to be. I have heard of doctors, lawyers, bankers, and accountants who have aspirations to drive truck someday.

In order to set reasonable goals we must first decide what goals we value. As significant an asset as education is, the lasting, rewarding values of life aren't found in a college curriculum.

Your children need to have the liberty to sort out their own aptitudes, skills, and interests. From my observation, those parents who set career goals for their children live to regret it.

A teacher shared with us an approach that worked in her experience. She first spent time listening to each student tell of his or her particular interests from early childhood. Then she worked at providing opportunities for each of them to participate in activities and studies related to those interests. Offering plenty of options and practical experiences seems to be the best way to guide children in making decisions regarding their future.

When I look at the large number of adults who eventually choose a career entirely different from the one they were trained for, I think something must be wrong with the way we are directing our young people.

Looking back, I can see more clearly what we should have aimed for. If I could start over today, my list would be something like this:

Let Them Share. Most children naturally tend to

share their toys and other belongings with their friends and neighbors, but parents stop them. Megan has six dolls and wants to give one to Amanda, who has only one of her own. Megan's parents think she is too young to make such a decision and don't allow her to give away her toys. She hasn't learned the value of hoarding yet, so her parents intervene.

I would model more sharing and give more freely to others. I'd also explain to my children the reasons for being generous, the value of a relaxed grasp on material possessions. But most of all, I'd take my hands off and let my children's generosity flow naturally.

Don't inhibit this virtue in your child.

Let Them Believe. More magic. More pretending. More spoofle dust. A few more wands, wishes, and what-ifs. We tended toward the more hard-nosed practical types. We wondered what use the imaginary had. We wanted everything to be real and true and tangible.

Our children could have taken us into the world of make-believe if we would have traveled with them, but we held back. We looked for the concrete. We weren't willing to let our feet leave the ground. We were practical Protestants.

But the land of make-believe is excellent territory to learn about faith. It's just a short hop, skip, and a jump from fairy godmothers and elves to guardian angels. We were afraid we couldn't teach the difference between the pretend and the real. Today I know we could have.

You have to believe before you can have faith. Children can move more easily into faith in Jesus Christ if the concept of believing is encouraged.

Children *can* understand the difference between the real and the imagined. We believe in fairies but they aren't real. We can close our eyes and make-believe we see them. There's nothing wrong with that.

We also believe in Jesus who is real. We believe in

angels; we close our eyes and picture them and they do exist.

Children often live in an imaginary world. But they also live in the real world and know the difference. The two worlds lend themselves to each other and neither need be a threat to the other.

When I was a child, we closed our eyes and tried to create our own world. Our imaginations conjured up all kinds of exotic animals and faraway lands we'd only read about in school. I wish we had also been encouraged to imagine what angels were up to, what heaven was like, and how God must look when He smiles.

Let Them Love. True expressions of love are too often neglected in the home. Our care and concern for the well-being of our kids can come across as a list of rules, an expectation of certain behavior, especially among Christians. I'm afraid it was that way at times in our home.

The best place for a child to be nurtured is at the knee or on the lap of an adult who hugs, kisses, smiles, and speaks words of tender encouragement. Children who miss this experience often spend decades looking for the real thing. Children don't learn love from a self-centered, self-righteous home.

My goal would be to show more affection to my children, to receive more from them. Allow yourself the pleasure of giving and receiving love. Be an example of a loving, understanding parent.

Expressing love and affection should come naturally, but it doesn't with many of us. The world has polluted demonstrations of affection so that many are afraid to show it to their children. Healthy expressions of love must be carefully cultivated in the home environment, so that children go out into the world with the right ideas about what love is, what it isn't, and how to demonstrate it to others.

I'd teach my children that love is something you give, not something you go out and get for yourself. My goal would be wholesome, generous love. I'd model and teach, but most of all I'd get out of the way and let it happen.

Let Them Trust. One of the greatest experiences in life is to have a child fall asleep on your lap, on your chest, or in your arms. There are things in life that are memorable, even exhilarating—climbing the Rockies, laughing past midnight with friends, hitting a home run. But a trusting child asleep in your arms is the ultimate.

Some parents actually train their children to distrust nearly everyone and every situation. Let your children learn the elementary principles of trust first.

People who trust get along better with God, their spouse, their friends, their pastor, and their doctor. In a world where trust is questioned, I'd like to see children experience the joy of putting their trust in someone.

To teach them more about trust, I'd

- let them jump off more kitchen counters into my waiting arms.
- hold them upside down in the living room and hear them laugh.
- encourage them to free-fall backward into my unseen, waiting arms.
- tell them I'd be by to pick them up at three o'clock and then be there on time.
- promise them ice cream for dessert and show up with a cold sack in my arms.
- tell them I'm taking them fishing and then keep my word.

In our day we have reason to be cautious and to teach children to be aware of strangers, but some parents seem to major in fear. They teach their children to be suspicious, to question every person's intentions, expect disasters and tragedies. Those are costly lessons. Constant fear is learned at the expense of simple trust.

If we don't teach trust to a child, where will he learn it? Grown-ups don't suddenly begin to trust people or their circumstances, much less God. People who are distrustful tend to remain that way for life.

Few people trust Jesus Christ who haven't first learned to trust a fellow human being. Trust cannot be grasped without experiencing it.

Trust is built over time. Thoughtful parents start stacking the building blocks of trust from an early age, so that when children are ready to be out on their own they have a good foundation of trust in humankind and a concept of what it is to trust God. The Bible teaches us:

Love always trusts (1 Corinthians 13:6–7).

Blessed is the one who trusts (Proverbs 16:20).

Trust can be misplaced (Psalm 20:7).

Joy and peace are a result of trust (Romans 15:13).

Trust is too vital to all of life to be omitted. Let's start teaching it to our children.

The Most Important Goals

The most important goals in life are often considered unusual, out of the ordinary. That's because they relate to developing inner qualities. These goals differ from how we normally measure success. If someone says, "I want my child to be a doctor," I wonder, "What kind of person will that doctor be?" If they want their child to be a pastor, I wonder the same thing.

When Mary was a senior in high school, she received an award from one of the service organizations in our town. As the school counselor presented the plaque, he said, "All parents would probably like to see their children grow up to be lawyers or be in some other prestigious profession, but mostly we want them to grow up to be good people. Today Mary gets this award because she is a good person.''

This represented a worthy goal in my estimation.

16

The Battle for the Supper Hour

Talk about lost causes. No one wants to advocate the impossible, but let this be one strong call for sanity. If there's any way for a family to preserve mealtime together, the effort will be well worth it.

Families of all sizes and lifestyles need a regular time when they sit down as a unit and face one another. If a family is assembled together, there's a possibility that communication might take place. But if no such gathering of family members occurs, it is virtually impossible for a family to share any meaningful exchanges.

Simply put, if we don't get together, we won't communicate. And if we don't get together for a meal, when in the world will we do it?

Loss of the family mealtime was one of the genuine tragedies at our house. Our children might not agree, but as they grew older they tended to see the supper hour as an intrusion into their otherwise active, hectic lives.

About the time they entered puberty the demands on their time mounted almost uncontrollably. Coaches, teachers, friends, youth workers, employers, and other parents seemed to have total disregard for the family supper hour. They had schedules, quotas, practices, and special events to be accomplished. How those pressures would affect a growing family apparently wasn't a major concern to the outside forces.

Like most families, ours was growing and changing. That rapid process frequently left us confused and in desperate need of some communication with our children. Unfortunately, we allowed ourselves to be robbed of the one time when any significant conversation might have taken place. Social forces were at work taking on a life of their own. We constantly struggled to resist those tides, and in the final analysis we didn't do too well.

TV Dinners

Morning is a frantic time when family members are rushing around looking for clean socks, toothpaste, schoolbooks, and car keys. Pit stops at the table are brief, punctuated by the morning news and the weather report on the TV. Then the anchorwoman explains how to get jelly stains out of a light-colored sweater. It's the American way—isn't it?

Frequently suppertime is equally kinetic. Does this picture sound familiar?

Junior has to eat early in order to make soccer practice. Sis will eat later, after band rehearsal. The message on the answering machine says not to expect Mom until around eight. (She has a part-time job in Butler County.) Dad is home on time tonight, but there's no one to eat with. Oh well, he has to leave in a few minutes anyway to pick up his new bowling ball.

Each member of the family finds whatever he can in the fridge or pantry and zaps it in the microwave. If they're lucky, Mom leaves a fresh casserole now and then.

More often than not, if there's any time at all to consume this plate of food, each family member finds his way into the family room to veg in front of the TV. That's dinner in a lot of our neighborhoods. Even if a family eats together, it is often in front of the TV, where disconnected family members eat, look straight ahead, and barely utter a word. Sound familiar? Many families might as well sell their dining room tables and buy another VCR.

When this scenario isn't the case, the family is eating out—not together in a restaurant—but dashing to a fast-food drive-thru and moving on to the next activity.

In the midst of such disarray come a few woeful cries: "I wish we had suppertime back." "If only we could sit around the table for just an hour a day and find out what's happening with everyone." "I'm getting tired of eating alone." "I'm getting sick of fast food."

The people we talked to who had grown children said if they had it to do over again they'd fight for the supper hour together. They agreed this fast-fading ancient custom was too valuable to lose—at least not without a fight.

Not Necessarily a Pleasant Time

We'd be remiss if we gave the impression that mealtimes are always or must always be pleasant times. The fact is, they can be miserable gatherings. We had friends in Detroit who regularly had supper separately—that is, Mom ate with the children and Dad ate alone. That was because he couldn't tolerate the bickering that accompanied the meal.

When the children are infants, meals tend toward chaos. Baby sits in the high chair, tosses his food around, drops his bowl, and bangs his spoon on the tray.

Grade-school children tease, insult each other, and kick siblings under the table during meals. They trade clever banter as soon as Mom gets up to refill a bowl. But—they also share moments of discovery, wonder, and excitement.

The doldrums move in with the teen years. This age group resembles a volcano. For weeks they sit silently, picking sullenly at their food. Then one day they suddenly erupt like Mt. St. Helen's, spewing accusations, denunciations, and proclamations in every direction. Both moods tend to be educational.

But—with all of this and more to contend with—veteran parents still agree eating supper together is worth it all! Mealtime can be the perfect occasion to get to know one another better. Passions frequently rush to the surface. Dreams have a way of rising through the fog. Compliments often sneak in when least expected.

Mealtime is when we learn one another's political persuasion. Many local and national leaders have been defended or defamed during the same meal in our dining room.

It's also the place where we have shared our faith—often inadvertently. We discuss where we think God fits into the total picture as well as in specific areas of our lives. Even the prayer of thanks before the meal has a unifying effect.

Members of minority groups have been defended over a loaf of freshly baked bread. Sometimes they ate the bread with us. Murderers have been condemned and even extolled at our table. Fads, single parents, teachers, clowns, fools, heroes, women's rights, the poor, and scores of other causes and personalities have been discussed, chewed up, and regurgitated over roast beef.

The Anvil of Values

Like smithies hammering in the livery, families work out, test, and refine their values as they break bread together. If we give up this roundtable of ideas, what will take its place? Is there some family experience waiting in the wings that we're ready to tie into?

How do my children know how I feel about abortion? We talked about it at the table. How do I know how my daughters feel about women ministers? They explained it to us as we passed carrots. How do I know where my children like to spend their vacations? They told me while we ate Reuben sandwiches.

Too many children have no concept of their parents' values. There are few settings where something this significant can be shared in an informal way. The forums for important ideas didn't begin in town meetings or at city councils. They were born at supper tables by family members who tested them on each other.

Breaking Bread

No doubt popping a meal into a microwave and grabbing your food as you run out the door has some social significance. It's convenient and it saves time.

The wonders of fast-food drive-thru lines definitely have had an impact on the family unit. If you can do it together all the better. And eating burgers in front of a rerun of *Gilligan's Island* has its small share of personal peace and pleasure. But the breaking of bread among family members and friends around a table still outweighs the benefits of any of the speedier methods.

It's not accidental that Jesus broke bread with his disciples. Nor was it mere chance that the early church frequently centered their fellowship and teaching ministries around the joys of passing food.

Food strengthens the body and enlivens the soul. Throughout the book of Acts the early Christians are

breaking bread and praying (2:42)
breaking bread in their homes (2:46)
coming together to break bread (20:7)
going upstairs to break bread (20:11)
taking bread and giving thanks (27:35).

What can take its place? Being together at mealtime is too special to give up completely simply because our lives have become too busy and fragmented.

Reading Around the Table

One of our best purchases was a hardback copy of *Little Visits With God*. At the time it was one of the best volumes of short, inspirational stories for children. Suppertime was the perfect place to share a few pages with Mary, Jim, and June.

In the early days our children were in no hurry to dash away from the table. As they grew older each one took turns reading as we passed a book around after the meal.

We were so pleasantly old-fashioned that no one could leave the table until they'd asked permission to do so. Our friends laughed at us for this prehistoric practice. But we still think it was a worthy attempt at maintaining some form of civility.

The supper hour was also a great time to share good stories. Each of us was encouraged to tell about something positive that happened during the day. Some whining and complaining was allowed, but we tried to keep it to a minimum.

Positive talk is as habit-forming as any other kind of speech. We felt that our children shouldn't be total strangers to the sound of uplifting conversation. And the supper table was a good place for them to hear it.

By the time all three of our kids were around high-school age, mealtime was straining at the seams. We couldn't hold on to the hour or the atmosphere. We're just glad we could keep it as long as we did.

Today Pat and I usually eat together, and we still enjoy the suppertime ritual. We almost always keep the television turned off while we eat, and we still drink each other in as part of the menu.

Holidays and special events are cherished now because our children and their families crowd around the same old table. Once again suppertime turns into an anvil of opinions, a drinking in of values and ideas, and a feast of joy.

17

Get Control of the Television

This chapter might surprise you. It might even be a disappointment, as I begin by telling you that I've never considered television to be the root of all evil. I even believe that television regularly contains some great moments for both the individual and the family.

We waste too much energy trying to blame our problems on a box that sits in our living room. There is a need to control this medium, but under the right conditions television can be a rich addition to a child's life.

Try saying this (at first it will stick in your throat, but don't give up): "Television is a gift from God." I have asked many groups to repeat this after me and there are always people who can't say it. The words turn to dust and dry up in the diaphragm.

Once a family accepts television as a gift from God, they can begin to deal with it. As long as they see it as a satanic box, there's no way to get a grip and master it.

I'd like to think our family was average when it came to viewing television, but there's no way to know for sure. Some of us almost never watched the tube; some watched quite a bit; and one or two turned it on only late at night (we didn't have cable when the children lived at home).

Because we were concerned, we tried to exercise a certain amount of monitoring, but that often led to bickering, complaining, and hot tempers.

Our Solution

The children used to beg to watch a program that we felt was laced with immorality. This comedy was off the wall, and the little we knew about it suggested the show was unfit for any age group.

Finally, to settle the issue, I came up with a scheme (I like schemes and often enjoyed trying them out on our children). I made up a test sheet and gave a copy to each member of the family. Listed on each sheet were twelve or fourteen categories.

The goal was to watch this menacing show together. Afterward, everyone was to grade the program from A to F in each of the categories on the sheet.

Some of the categories were the regular run of the mill: language, sex, and violence. Others focused on caring, helpfulness, loyalty, and love. Were kind acts of friendship and good values being expressed? Did the characters make you laugh or cry? After watching did you feel better or worse about yourself?

Each member of the family had a test sheet and a pencil. We watched the show together and graded it intently. When the program was over we turned the set off and tallied the results.

To our surprise, the show that had held our home in a grip of tension turned out to be a pussycat. The characters were funny, they obviously cared very much for each other, and were never mean or ugly-spirited.

Often their humor appeared to put other people down, but only in a superficial way. Almost never did they try to hurt one another and never did they act seriously offended. They never cut to the quick and always rebounded to help each other.

Now this show wasn't exactly the Gospel of John, but neither was it horrible. Viewers had to keep their perspective, but nothing in the sitcom appeared damaging.

Result: The show got a B. A strong B, I might add. We never again complained about the show and often watched it with the children.

The kids were right (I can't believe I'm saying this). Our children were right.

Always one to drive a good thing into the ground, I made up more evaluation sheets. Some categories were expanded or condensed, but basically it was the same test we used the first time.

We turned television testing into a sport. Anyone could choose a show and we'd attack the project with vigor. Comedies, musicals, educational shows, dramas—they were all fair game for this hunt. We were watching television together as a family and we were interacting!

Finally we had our own findings to discuss. We weren't going to take someone else's word for what was acceptable or unacceptable.

This experiment enabled our family to make intelligent judgment calls. One program may have been deemed sleazy and worthless while another was discovered to have far more redeeming qualities than we could have imagined. We weren't looking for perfect programs. We weren't fine-tooth combing over a word or two that might offend us. Our goal was to discover the overall value of the program.

Television was becoming educational for us, in spite of itself.

More Than Victims

The children who suffer most from watching television are those who are allowed to watch it without reservation. Sitting in front of the set and inviting shows to pour worthless or damaging material into your passive brain might turn you into a Frankenstein.

An important key is to rise above being a victim. Television can't dictate to you and your children without being challenged. Thinking children and adults can make television work to their advantage.

Television probably ranks among the top five most significant influences in our lives. Whether that fact frightens us or brings us pleasure depends on our ability to rise above the level of being a victim.

Taking Control

Here are a few simple steps that will make family viewing profitable. Pick and choose which ones fit your situation.

Step One. Make a schedule. Let children choose programs ahead of time instead of watching randomly and endlessly.

Step Two. Limit how many hours small children can watch the set on a given evening.

Step Three. Watch programs as a family. Any negative impact may be greatly reduced if others are in the room.

Step Four. Make trades. This takes some work but it's worth it. Examples: One hour of homework gets an hour and a half of television. One hour of reading earns two hours in front of the set. Don't be afraid to make deals.

Step Five. Create test sheets and begin evaluating programs as a family.

Step Six. Refuse to use television as a baby-sitter or to keep the children out of your hair.

Make up your own steps. Get involved. Put your God-given creative mind to work and get a handle on the problem.

A friend tells of a time when he paid his children a dollar a day not to watch television. They gladly took the money and gradually developed other interests. After the father removed the reward, each of the children established their own watching habits.

Another father felt that a parent's involvement with the children was the best remedy for too much television. If parents will play on the floor with their children or take them outside and do things together, they help create a lifestyle that isn't dependent on the tube.

A healthy approach to television viewing takes time and involvement, but the alternative is to let television and its effects rule the house.

You Can't Get Rid of It

Every once in a while we hear of a family who has thrown their television set out. Now they live happily doing woodworking projects, reading stacks of books together, and spending hours hiking or bird-watching.

We are happy for those families, but unfortunately that won't happen for most of us. Television sets are like boomerangs. Even if you throw them away they have a way of coming back. One reason is because there *are* some good things on TV.

Twice we went without television. It's true that we read more, walked more, and saw more Baltimore Orioles flitting from tree to tree.

And both times someone felt sorry for our family and *gave* us a television set. Being the fallen creatures we are, we accepted the 19-inch fruits.

Families without television tend to lose their children to other families. As soon as supper is over, they head for the neighbors' to "get help with their homework." While parents naively think their children are poring over Napoleon's battles, measuring iambic pentameter, or discussing relativity, they are in actuality watching reruns of *The Brady Bunch* (the clue is they are humming the theme song on the way in your door).

Keep your children at home. Get a handle on television. Separate the good fruit from the bad and learn to tell the difference.

This Gift From God

While watching the TV news one evening, God moved me to get involved with a refugee family. If I couldn't help all Asians, I could at least reach out to one family.

I can remember a time when our family was especially tense. To get some relief, we sat down and watched a family comedy. We laughed, relaxed, and hoped again.

On an educational channel we watched conception take place and the early stages of a baby's development in a mother's womb. We marveled at the miracle and God's design.

My friend was watching a television show when the

Lord convicted him then and there of his sins. In that moment he gave his life to Jesus Christ.

There are ways to take control of the television set. Learn how to handle your gift from God.

18

Share and Pray

The meeting was scheduled for 7:00 P.M. in the living room. Each of us was supposed to bring something to share. The children were grade-school age and their parents were plenty old enough.

The minute we made the announcement, the family stampeded throughout the house. Mary rifled through an old toy box. Jim began thumbing around in the record and tape collection. June headed for Pat's Sunday school and education files.

When the big hand hit twelve our quintet sat around the room holding whatever object lesson or book they had chosen to bring. This was show-and-tell on a spiritual level.

Everybody had a turn to fill the room with creativity. Jim moved the couch and placed a record player behind it. Arm stretched high above the back of the couch, he led us in a song with a puppet on his hand and music playing in the background.

Next, June hung a flannel cloth over the back of that same couch. Then in her most innovative style she told us a Bible story, complete with sound effects.

Mary put on a play with toys on the floor. Pat read a two-page story from a book. I read a Proverb or a short story that Christ had told.

We ended our time together talking to the Lord about our dreams, our hopes, our fears.

These sessions continued once a week for some time at the Coleman house. No one seemed to be bored. We didn't have to threaten anyone to get the family together. We shared, we participated, we had a good time, and we learned about the love of God.

I miss those times together. They can never happen again—not the way they were. That thought feels good and hurts at the same time. I think it's called a bitter-sweet memory.

Mashed Potato Devotions

At first we tried the staid approach. I vividly remember sitting with two-year-old Mary in the kitchen. She was in her high chair, I was sitting close by, my open Bible in hand.

Anxious to get on with her formal Bible training, I was reading from the book of Obadiah.

"Shall I not in that day, saith the Lord, even destroy the wise men out of Edom, and understanding out of the mount of Esau? And thy mighty men, O Teman, shall be dismayed, to the end that every one of the mount of Esau may be cut off by slaughter" (1:8–9, KJV).

As I looked up at our innocent little toddler, she looked back at me. Her cheeks bulged with food and mashed potatoes oozed between the fingers of her tiny fists.

I burst out laughing at the outrageous scene. I could almost hear God and three cloud-loads of angels laughing with me.

The mashed potato queen didn't really care about Edom, Esau, or the warriors of Teman. But if it made her father happy, she was willing to listen.

That's when I regrouped. Like so many other parents I decided to make Bible reading simple and directed at my children's level.

Our children taught us to get on their level or give it up. Bible reading had to become more than a dad's duty. What value was there in reading to the children merely to satisfy my sense of parental obligation? I needed to communicate to them.

Done correctly, family quiet times can lead to great communication. One friend told us that open discussion was one of the greatest benefits of having devotions with her four children.

Often they shared and prayed together at mealtime. These sessions frequently led into terrific conversations that lasted well into the evening.

Feeling Obligated

Like many Christians I had come to accept a daily quiet time or a devotional time as one of life's great guilt trips. For me it always tended toward legalism—a "God is going to get you if you don't take time out for Him" feeling to it. I wish I'd seen it more as an opportunity to meet with our heavenly Father.

Pass on a sense of genuine Christian spirituality to your children. They need to know the power and presence of the Holy Spirit, not merely learn the rules and regimen placed on them by others.

Devotional times can impart the following to your children:

1. They can get a sense of security in knowing that this family trusts God; they have a feeling of being in God's care.

2. It provides the joy of learning on a daily basis.

3. It guides children in their everyday encounters; it helps them to make wise choices.

4. It is a part of their total care, just as food, shelter, and clothing are provided for them.

As the children became teenagers we backed off from a formal setting for devotions. After Mary left for college we gave up regular readings at the table. Jim was off wrestling and running cross-country. June was busy in theater and leading the marching band.

That was all right. It was time for their connection with the Lord to become more of an individual and personal matter. From time to time I noticed their marked Bibles and other Christian materials in their rooms. Today it's a decision they must make for themselves and their own families. We're content to leave those choices with them.

Parents' Frustration

Often Christian parents have this dilemma. How do they share a sense of spirituality in a way that is meaningful and yet not mechanical? How can they establish a method without turning off their children and chasing them away from a relationship with Christ?

The number one way is to model your faith in front of your children. Living out the basics of trust, forgiveness, tolerance, and love will have a more profound effect on your family than all of the booklets, devotionals, and meditations you could ever use.

Children need to see that faith does not reside in a book or in a building. Faith resides in people and those people are, first of all, their parents. Whatever they see in your daily lives will speak more loudly than any routine you can develop.

When asked how they demonstrate faith to their children, parents often reply that they go to church. It's a big mistake to think that church attendance is a sign of your faith. Church attendance may help strengthen and fortify your faith, but don't ever think it takes its place.

Our faith in Christ manifests itself in the way it changes our personalities and deportment.

I wish I'd shown our children more of the grace of God in my life. It was there. I simply wish they could have seen more of the process that God was bringing about in me as He continued to adjust my attitude, my values, and my behavior.

Pray to Change

Only recently have I learned that I need to pray in order to change *me*. I wish I'd known it when our children were preschoolers.

I spent too much time praying that my children would change. In those days I often used prayer to try to manipulate others. Now I've come to see the relative foolishness of this. I wish I'd spent more time praying for changes in myself instead.

There is no way to produce spiritual life in children. The best we can do is to provide an atmosphere where spiritual life can occur and grow. Parents are the key to that atmosphere.

Great Materials to Choose From

When our children were in grade school, materials to use at home weren't nearly as prolific as they are today. Now bookstores have a wide variety of excellent books, Christian music, and other materials for families. We found a couple of books geared to the very young, but not many. That's when we began to write our own materials.

Our children were interested in animals and nature. I noticed the Bible makes many references to nature. Christ told stories about sheep, foxes, wolves, flowers, trees, and seeds. Soon I was writing nature stories for our children. Eventually these tales turned into five or six books on nature and the Bible.

Smart parents look for a way to develop their child's ordinary interests and use them to build a bridge to the Bible. If your children enjoy stars and constellations or history or people, take those subjects and use them to introduce them to Bible characters, stories, and principles.

Parents need to be personal and creative in using attention grabbers that appeal to their children.

Not a Weapon

Desperate for any device that will help, parents are too often prone to use God as a weapon to discipline their children. Do parents still say, "God is going to get you for that" or, "I'm going to spank you because God is unhappy with what you've done"?

It's a big mistake to use the Lord as a paddle to get your children moving, presenting an image of God that is a big bad ogre. Parents drive their children away from God by using such archaic practices.

Our heavenly Father is accepting, loving, and merciful. We do everyone a disfavor by pointing to a bogeyman in the sky.

However, we shouldn't be too surprised if we fail to give an exact representation of God to our children. If you're like me, you're still grappling with spiritual concepts and still learning what God is like yourself.

Since our spiritual journey is not yet complete,

maybe we need to be simple and humble with the way we represent God to our children. A little less dogma, a tad fewer rules, and a lot more love and compassion might be in order.

Worth the Effort

When good parents realize how vital it is to spend devotional time with their children, they often go to great lengths to make it happen. A young father who managed a small assembly plant often had to work overtime. Sometimes his workload kept him away from the family too much.

To rectify the situation, this father began to get up and go to work at 4:00 A.M. That allowed him to set up for the day and then hurry home for breakfast with his family.

This gave him genuine quality time with his children before they went to school. In the summer he always came home for lunch.

There's too much to share and too much to pray about to ignore these gatherings. They're rare treasures to cherish while they last.

19

The Almighty Dollar

It's almost as hard to talk about money as it is to talk about God or sex. Maybe parents feel guilty or protective or confused about their attitude toward filthy lucre.

If we're confused about our feelings regarding money, we're apt to pass confusion on to our children. They may believe money has a mysterious, powerful, even dangerous aura about it. Like drugs, money can make people euphoric or despondent or addicted. Children pick up on that and stand in awe at the mystical dynamics of cash, credit, checks, spending, and saving.

College and Cash

One of the most daring reality checks we made with our children was when we told them they'd be responsible for half of their college expenses. Pat and I didn't come to that decision easily, but we became convinced it was the best way to help our children. We told them plenty early so they could start to put their bucks in a row.

Before we reached that decision we talked to friends about their college experiences. One woman told us, "My dad simply handed me a checkbook. He could easily afford it. Whatever it cost for tuition or books or room and board, I'd simply write a check for that amount. It was nice, but I know there was a lot I didn't learn that way."

From our own experience, we learned that the times we had part-time jobs in college were the times we did the best academically. Too much time on our hands tended to make us careless and inattentive.

Every dollar our kids raised would be matched with a dollar from us. Any scholarship money they earned (and scholarships could be dug up) went entirely onto their side of the ledger.

We said early on: You have several years to make plans. Decide what you want to do; decide where you want to go. If the school is expensive, decide whether or not you can afford to pay half.

Naturally our plan wasn't totally selfless. We knew we could afford to send one child to college. However, two years into the program the second one would be college-bound, followed closely by the third. We didn't know if we could sustain the entire flock.

Making this kind of decision takes courage. There's no neat package of right and wrong. Our decision was based on wanting to spread the responsibility and, basically, it worked.

Today we can't say we sent our kids to college. We helped send them to college. They played major roles in financing their educational process. One child graduated without any one of us owing a dime. The other two could have, too.

When we first explained the funding program, Mary ran out and got a part-time job. The words "you're responsible" hit home and she decided to start pumping up her savings account. The other two children had longer to wait, but they started to plan.

How did our children feel about the matching challenge? Will they do the same with their kids? We don't know and really don't care. We needed to make a decision in our time and in our circumstances. Given that same mix, we'd do it again.

Parents need to make decisions and see them through. If we are racked by indecision and controlled by guilt, we make life miserable for everyone.

Malcolm MacGregor, an accountant, used to say that parents should look at community or junior colleges first. Since it takes so long for most students to select a major, why not go to school nearby? It's a cheaper education and places less of a burden on everyone.

Parents shouldn't be afraid to innovate. Conformity is no answer. Adults know that and yet often want their children to have precisely what everyone else has.

It was interesting to watch the families in our community handle their children's college finances. Some of the apparently well-to-do families shifted almost all of the responsibility for expenses onto their children. On the other hand, a few of the less affluent families paid every dime of the way.

There are many ways to handle the issue, but sharing the load has definite benefits for everyone.

No Guarantees

Parents can expose their children to good financial influences as they teach, model, share, and discuss, but eventually a child must develop and live by his own financial values.

Some children who are taught to save become big spenders. Families who avoid credit cards like the plague might produce offspring who go through them like chocolate.

One of our children kept a paper route for four years. Our rule was that half of the income had to be saved and half could be spent. He could reap immediate benefits and at the same time learn the rewards of squirreling something away.

We were pleased to watch the seeds of frugality take root. Our offspring seemed to take pleasure in the accomplishments that hard work could bring.

Eventually we said the money could be taken out for any cause he considered. Almost overnight the sizable nest egg vanished.

Today I wonder if our carefully managed savings program was worth anything to our son. But the lessons derived from saving are important and should be shared as long as you forget guarantees. Expose children to a variety of wise options and leave it with the Lord. Each child must create his own system and follow that system to his own profit or loss.

Getting Involved

Be actively involved with your child's income and expenses.

- Help them set goals for bikes, cars, or other large purchases. Explain how much (if any) you'll contribute to the purchase. When the child earns the balance, the merchandise becomes his.
- How much will you spend for a pair of jeans? If she wants designer ones, let her dig up the cash for part of the cost.
- If a teen needs money for the big date or big event, let him know well in advance if you plan to help. This gives him an idea of how much he needs to

save. Waiting, planning, and saving are good experiences for all.

- Help your child find a job. At first it can be an especially scary adventure. Give him hints on how to get a paper route or show him how to read the Classifieds.
- Look for financial experiences to share with your children. Words and warnings aren't enough.
- Give your children some idea of how you handle giving. How do you decide what to donate to the church, missions, hunger relief, or whatever? They need a frame of reference.

Biblical Attitudes

The Scriptures make no attempt to dictate all our financial moves. But the Bible is big on attitudes. It warns us against loving money (1 Timothy 6:10), against greediness (1 Peter 5:2), against serving money (Matthew 6:24); it tells us how to give money cheerfully (2 Corinthians 9:7), and even warns us against saving too much (Luke 12:13–21).

Attitudes! Watch how you relate to money. Let it serve you, don't serve it. And pass on those attitudes to your children.

Teach Them to Give

We tried to draw short straight lines between our gifts and how they were used. In many large churches children give their dollars with only a vague concept of what the money goes for. A large percentage of it might go for air-conditioning or heating, or the general budget of the church. Children don't understand the connection between their offering of sacrifice and the church's institutional needs. If you want to help them give to a particular ministry or missionary, be sure you see that it is channeled that way.

When our children were in elementary school, we signed up to help support a foreign child. Our family sent a set amount of money each month and in return received a small photo and an occasional letter. The letters helped make the child become a real person to us. Our children could identify better with a child in need than asphalt paving for the church parking lot.

If we teach children to simply hoard money in their piggy banks, they are only getting a lesson in self-centeredness. If we show them how to spend it all on themselves, we demonstrate the art of self-indulgence. But what about showing them how to spread their money around to help others? Then we've communicated the lesson of sharing and turning paper dollars into life-changing properties.

Sending twenty dollars in the mail to a friend or even a stranger at the right time, paying a bill for someone, or giving a coat to a needy child are actions that demonstrate the true power of money.

We often gave our offerings without including our children in the process. In our more thoughtful moments, we let the children contribute a dime, a quarter, or a dollar to a good cause. It's good for children to watch their dollars educate, feed, clothe, or simply encourage another human being.

When a local mission runs an ad in the paper explaining how they can feed a good meal to a dozen people for $25.00, you can help your children participate in the process of transforming money into food for hungry people by offering to double or triple what they can give to help the cause.

Many think that controlling a child's money is the best way to teach financial management. It's far more valuable to teach the joy of giving. We aren't talking about large gifts or contributing to unknown institutions where money is lost in the paperwork. We want to emphasize compassion. People helping people is close to the heart and ministry of Jesus Christ.

If your children see the example of generosity and choose to reject it, that's their decision. At least they should be given the opportunity of seeing the spirit of giving in action.

The principles of Christian sharing are best understood when we see them for ourselves. Parents paint pictures with their actions. One act of sharing is worth a thousand sermons and lectures on giving.

The apostle Paul, speaking of God's generosity, quotes the psalmist, "He has scattered abroad his gifts to the poor; his righteousness endures forever" (2 Corinthians 9:9).

Key Issues

Instead of being bewildered by money, children should be exposed to its full potential—both for good and for harm.

Generally money should go in three directions. It should be

saved

spent

given away.

Every person must develop his own plan of accomplishing this, but each element should be included. An extreme in any direction will put money outside the realm of its intended use.

Saving it all, spending it all, or giving it all away leads to an unbalanced life. The Lord of your child's life is also the Lord of your child's finances. Finances are not his security. The only real security is in Jesus Christ.

With these values in mind, you can better direct your children into the skill of money management before they have to make financial decisions on their own.

20

Let Them Argue More

I wish I knew then what I know now about a scenario common to many families. Many years passed before I got a clue.

Big brother Jim would be playing with little sister June. Before too long we'd hear a blood-curdling scream. Protective parents that we were, we rushed to save our beleaguered little girl. Sure as anything, June would be in tears and Jim would be staring at the floor in disgust.

We'd haul Jim out of the room and either confine him to his bedroom or take privileges away. Strict, all-knowing parents like us weren't about to let "Jim the bully" pick on innocent, charming June.

This scenario was played out so often we almost came to accept it as a family tradition. June screamed; we rushed in like firefighters and carried Jim out by the armpits.

Why did Jim enjoy picking on his sister so much? We pulled our hair out, read books and articles, lay prostrate on the floor waiting for answers from above.

Finally the answer came like a lightning bolt from

heaven. Watching the two of them play from afar, we finally discovered what was going on.

June would yank a toy out of Jim's hands or gouge him in the eyes. In self-defense, Jim would whack her one in return. June would then go directly for an Oscar. Screaming at a glass-shattering pitch, her wail for help rippled through the house. Two seconds later she'd hear the thundering hoofbeats of her parents galloping to her rescue. Nostrils flared, faces red, they scooped up their terrorist son and whisked him away to certain torture and deprivation.

Only after months of playing posse did we figure out the problem. We were impounding the wrong kid.

And today we know the same conspiracy is widespread. Younger siblings all over the country with cherub-like dimples are doing in older brothers and sisters while their parents give unsuspecting enablement.

I wish we knew then what we know now. That's why we share it with you here. Most parents don't learn the truth until it's too late.

Normally parents are highly protective of the atmosphere. We want peace and harmony in our homes. So much is our desire for tranquillity that we're willing to rant, rave, and go to extremes to get it. There's no end to the cacophony parents are willing to raise in order to establish a semblance of peace.

In pursuit of this we often miss an essential ingredient. Our children *need* to argue and squabble among themselves.

"What?" you may be saying.

That's right. Learning to argue with peers and siblings is one of the important foundations of maturity. Giving, taking, winning, losing, presenting one's case, showing one's logic, coping with threats, and recovering to argue again are merely a few of the personality strengths every child needs to develop.

If we deny them the opportunity by constantly inter-
vening, we slow the maturing process. Children will
have to develop those skills somewhere, somehow. A
few never will acquire them adequately.

Parents plead in desperation, "Why do our children
fight all the time?"

The answer is, "Because they're trying to grow up."

If they can argue under the right conditions with the
proper limits in place, they'll grow up better balanced.

What's a Fair Fight?

I asked one mother if she left her eight-year-old and
nineteen-year-old daughters alone to settle their arguments.

"Of course," she answered.

"Don't you think it's unfair, considering the large age
difference between them?" I asked.

"Oh, I grant you the nineteen-year-old is at a considerable disadvantage, but I leave them to it anyway."

Innocent eyes, disarming dimples, blushing cheeks,
and a quiet voice tell us nothing about a child's abilities
in jaw-to-jaw combat. Behind that soft look there's usually a fantastically creative mind processing the chal-
lenges she will throw at her older sibling.

After establishing two guidelines for sibling rivalry,
remove yourself from the arena. They need the freedom
to settle their own disputes:

1. No hitting or other physical abuse.

2. No use of language already understood as off-limits
for this family in this home.

Parents are anxious to create fair playing fields for
their children. This desire is a loving one but is often
misguided.

When your kids go to the church nursery or playschool, their fights won't be fair or on an equal basis. Some pushy kid will try to get the green stuffed dinosaur away from your child, and no one will be there to keep things fair and even for your child.

In high school, some great-looking teen will try to steal their date away. They won't be able to go to the date monitor and demand fairness.

When they get a job in this wayward world, they'll likely cross paths with an arrogant, socially maladjusted, unreasonable fellow employee—and the personnel department won't have a kindness patrol.

In their hour of need our children will reach back into their mental bank and remember an overbearing sibling. They'll recall what they did to get Bunky to share his gumballs. They'll rely on the same tactics that persuaded Sissy to hand over her favorite sweater for the evening. Mustering up these childhood resources will help them not only survive, but prosper.

Football Negotiations

One Sunday afternoon I was throwing a football with my son and a few of his grade-school friends in our backyard. As we tossed the ball around, the brother of one of the boys rode up on his bike.

Hopping off, he said, "Here, let me throw it."

His brother snapped back, "No. Get out of here. We don't want you to play."

Instinctively, I moved toward them about to give my "it's only fair to let everyone have a turn" sermonette. Before I got very far the newest arrival responded to his brother.

"If you don't let me play I'm going to tell Mom what you did."

"What was that?" the brother with the ball snarled.

New-arrival-brother whispered into his ear.

"All right," said the boy with the ball, "you can have a few throws." And the football changed hands.

The wonders wrought by finely honed negotiating skills and the marvel of it all. No one even asked me to give my fairness speech.

Parental Interference

"If we don't intercede, our children will never learn fairness," one parent objected.

The exact opposite is more likely to be the case. There *are* a few referees of fairness in life and we're grateful for them. But most of life comes without a hall monitor. We have to learn to wriggle through the corridors and climb the staircases of life for ourselves.

Parents can give their children two great gifts to make this walk easier.

1. Teach them to be fair.

2. Let them work out their arguments with their siblings in order to practice what we teach.

The Fairness Illusion

Children who are allowed to argue with siblings, friends, neighbors, and the deacon's kids are certain to learn one of the basic principles for living: Life isn't fair.

Tyler *did* eat more than half of the candy. This *is* Ashley's second time to stay up late. Zach *did* get to pick the television show last night. Megan *had* the red sled last time, too.

As they argue over each of those vital issues, they'll learn through experience that life isn't fair. When Mom or Dad doesn't race over to measure each serving of nachos, they'll again realize that life isn't always measured out equally for all. After they win a few and lose a few, they'll soon discover that life was never intended to be fair. You can't win every time.

Then as teenagers and as adults they won't be devastated when they don't get what they thought they had coming. It was a lesson they learned back when Josh got the biggest piece of pizza two weeks in a row.

21

We'd Play More Games

Some of the parents we talked to said they simply weren't game people. They didn't enjoy getting on the floor, sitting around a game table, or romping around a park. For some reason they didn't care for the challenge of give-and-take in a playful manner.

Many others look back with fondness on the hours they spent in gentle competition with their children. They enjoyed the laughter. They cherish the image of their bright-eyed child thinking through a problem or obstacle course. They were proud when their son or daughter solved the puzzle, won the game, or lost good-naturedly.

Game-playing, indoors and out, is the clay from which pleasant memories are shaped. Now that our children are no longer living at home, we often long for the evenings when we would shuffle the cards, pull out the chess set, start a jigsaw puzzle, or spread another board game on the table.

Temperamental Players

If some of us had it to do again, we probably wouldn't play with such a cutthroat attitude. Not that we'd let our children win every game, but we wouldn't be afraid to lose either.

Playing games involves more strategy than that of the game itself. If we let Junior win, he may get a false sense of his ability. And if he eventually discovers Dad has been faking it, he might resent his parent's proclivity to give in so easily. Yet if a parent continuously wins, the child may lose all desire to play.

Select games your children can reasonably participate in and then play with them at a safe speed. They will learn as they go and adapt along the way to the gist of the game. You want to build their self-confidence, not yours.

We used to play a card game we called Nertz. In reality it's double solitaire with a considerable competitive edge. If you'll allow me to boast, I play it rather well. I have honed my skill on both children and adults.

However—seldom will anyone play this game with me today. Everyone leaves the room if I even mention it. Occasionally one of my grown children, out of sheer kindness, will volunteer to play it with me during the holidays. After a few beatings in succession, my opponent remembers a pot she must tend to on the stove or imagines a crying baby in need of her care. There's no moderate speed at which I can play this fast-paced game. Consequently I'm left alone and friendless.

Parents should refrain from playing games like this in which they continuously blow their kids out of the water. The child will either dwindle to despair or learn to win at all costs and become overbearing just like his mom or dad.

In our study of adult children we discovered that one

of the main reasons they didn't like to return home for holidays was because they knew an aging parent was waiting in the wings with a killer game at the ready.

It's an easy trap to get caught in if we aren't sensitive and careful. If I could do it over, I'd avoid the controlling attitude that says I must play my game. (At least I hope I would.)

A Key to Communication

For many families, playing board games is one of the easiest and most nonthreatening ways to communicate. For hours at a time family members can sit around a table in easy companionship. In between plays most tend to share what's on their heart and mind, what's been going on in their lives.

There's no pressure to "tell me what's going on," and yet the opportunity is available. Short questions. Brief answers. A relaxed atmosphere. No confrontation. Dialogue takes on a normal tone without becoming a major debate.

Relaxed games that don't consume all our energy with the immediate challenge allow time for thought between turns and ease in conversation.

Someone thinks of a joke to share or a bit of news from college. Even games that call for a considerable degree of concentration are best broken up with casual comments.

Not every game lends itself to communication, of course. Some are designed for speed, noise, or fierce competition. These can be good family games, too. They break the ice between siblings who have had some problems with each other, and get everyone to lighten up and enjoy one another's company.

Guidelines for Game Players

Family members should be able to compete with one another without doing damage to each other's psyche. When we play competitive games, we should keep a few guidelines in mind.

1. *Do or Die Won't Do.*

The family member who has to win (or else!) is someone who must be reasoned with. It may be a parent or it may be a child. Males seem to show a stronger driving force in this area and their egos are more fragile, of course.

Adults who feel they *must* beat their children at board games should find professional help. They are hurting themselves and other family members.

2. *My Game or Else.*

People who demand their own way in choosing a game or in interpreting the rules show antisocial behavior.

Brad was the kind of kid who was allowed to control his family. If someone wanted to play, Brad insisted on naming the game. Anxious to have his company, everyone gave in. If he started to lose, Brad threatened to quit. In order to keep the "family" game going, parents and siblings helped him become more successful.

Brad's family saw this as their attempt to create togetherness. In reality they were supporting a dictatorship where eleven-year-old Brad was the head honcho. Ultimately they did everyone a disservice.

Games have to be democratic. There's no room for four- or forty-year-old tyrants.

3. *Across the Ages.*

An adult who can't color with his five-year-old probably isn't ready to play family games. Parents who teach their six-year-old to play chess should stop and reassess their actions.

Too often, I wanted the children to be part of my world when I wasn't willing to be a part of theirs. Parents who can't bring themselves to play blocks haven't earned the right to ask a child to participate in a "more sophisticated game." If we can't get on the floor and play on his or her level, we can't expect a child to sit at a table and play on our level.

4. *Accepting Rejection.*

Dad yells out the invitation, "Who wants to play a game?"

The room remains silent. Susie is playing dolls. Tyler is working at the computer. Mom is reading a book.

"Hey, come on. It'll be fun," Dad pushes.

Still, there are no takers.

Dad slumps back onto the couch and pushes out his bottom lip. The invitation to play games has been rejected, and Dad is taking it personally.

I've done this, so I know what I'm talking about. Any adult who feels shunned when no one wants to play with him or her needs to get a grip. They are raising the stakes too high. A game is not a referendum on our personal value. That's why we call them games.

Sometimes the family just doesn't want to play at that time. Consequently, we need to look around for something else to do. "I don't want to play" doesn't mean "I don't like you." Fifth-graders may think so, but we adults should be mature enough to know the difference. If our children see us accept a no without a pout, they are more likely to accept rejection and bounce back into mature behavior themselves.

When handled correctly, family games provide healthy interaction among members. They provide fun times to be sure, but their value is far greater than fun times. The enjoyment that comes from playing games together gives birth to lifelong benefits.

22

Graduation Time

Eventually the time will come when parents find themselves sitting in an overcrowded, overheated auditorium to watch a graduation ceremony. This event is one of life's special rewards. We used to wonder if it would ever happen. Eighteen years seems like a long time when you're in the middle of it.

The day does finally arrive. It's a rite of passage. Remember the toddler next door you used to baby-sit once a week? He's wearing a cap and gown now. And the same girl who lifted her skirt at the first-grade Christmas program is graduating with honors.

Even the most stoic parent will struggle to hold back tears. Nostalgic reflections are bound to tug at our hearts (weddings, births, and college graduations will later thicken the lump in our throats).

Sitting there listening to the processional music, parents ponder what has now become history. You instilled some good traits into your child's life (and maybe a few that weren't so good). Those qualities have mixed with your child's own personality, influences of his or her broader environment, and then were tempered with a large dose of the grace of God.

For almost two decades this "pot" has been stirred regularly. Today the stew is about to be served. Most parents agree that raising children has been a satisfying experience. They aren't about to do it over again—but it was good. Their hearts are full of pride, and of praise to God.

Thank God for the privilege of raising a child. Thank God for a baby who sleeps in your arms, for a toddler whose smile is a tonic for your heart, for a schoolkid to play ball with in the park, for a teenager who wants to talk at 2:00 A.M., and for a young adult who isn't afraid to express his or her love to you.

Most parents will look back and remember the good times. The bad times become a blur. They know their life has been enriched by their children. And one day soon, they'll walk out into the backyard, look up at the open skies, and thank God for allowing children into their lives, even if only for a season.